THE DAY MY NIPPLE FELL OFF

and Other Stories
of Survival,
Solidarity, and Sass

A BAYS ANTHOLOGY

Edited by Erin Hyman

"The unifying theme is resilience and faith. The unifying theme is being a warrior and a motherfucker. It is not fragility. It's strength. It's nerve. And 'if your nerve deny you,' as Emily Dickinson wrote, 'go above your nerve'... I want to know what you have inside you. I want to see the contours of your second beating heart. So write... Not like a girl. Not like a boy. Write like a motherfucker."

—Cheryl Strayed, from *Tiny Beautiful Things*

Contents

III. Navigating Relationships

IV. Grief and Gratitude

Introduction

Erin Hyman
February 2013

Before I went to my first BAYS meeting, my only experience with support groups was in seeing them parodied in film or on TV. I had vague apprehensions about being subjected to tuna casserole, oversharing, or pious invocations of Jesus. What I got instead was a room full of bad-ass women, who—instead of simply being out in the world scaling mountains, brokering deals, dancing on bars, or mothering babes—were doing all those things while recovering from surgery, undergoing chemotherapy, or fending off the symptoms of hormone treatment. To paraphrase Woody Allen—or rather, to turn his saying about membership on its head—it was a club you never wanted to be a part of, but you were *damn* glad they'd have you as a member.

We are yoga teachers and financial planners, bikers and baristas, sex workers and nurse practitioners, lesbians and single moms, athletes and activists, students and teachers, doctors and patients. We speak many languages, hail from all over the world, and now call the San Francisco Bay Area home.

But the unfortunate and infuriating thing that unites us is being diagnosed with breast cancer in our thirties and forties, and for many, even twenties. BAYS gives us a place where we can ask any question, no matter how intimate or intimidating, and get answers, where we can share scars and scares, where we crack each other up and let each other cry.

What our meetings have shown me, reminded me, really, is how powerful our stories are. For each new member coming to their first meeting, or logging on to our list-serve for the first time, other people's stories are a lamp that lights the path ahead. They don't just illuminate what to expect when we're facing a procedure or starting a new drug, they show us that it's possible to move forward through the morass of cancer bullshit with humor, generosity, and chutzpah. Not to mention grace. Hearing that we are not hallucinating that side effect or that we are not wrong to weed out false friends, that our hair will return and our sex drives too—these are invaluable glimpses of the futures we are forging for ourselves through a swamp of unknowns.

Writing connects us. Many of us update blogs to keep the communities of loved ones around us apprised of what's happening, but we also find that the writing itself is sustaining. Our fears have cracked us open, and we pour our hearts out on the page. Our words show we are fierce and funny, and that cancer will not turn us into ghosts of ourselves.

By collecting some of these stories in print, I hoped to create a portable support group—a source to have at one's bedside, to reach for in moments when you need that voice of someone who's been there. It was inspired by an online post by IPJ, titled "Super-Sad, Sweet (Hopefully) Love Story," where she shared a moment both horrible and hilarious about her dating life. Reading it, I thought about the power of black humor, but also of the many things women in our situation have to contend with that are not the usual fare of cancer-self-help literature: What is it like to tell someone you're dating that cancer has put you in menopause? To explain to your inquiring preschooler why you no longer need a bra? To attend a high-school reunion post-chemo and acknowledge your changed appearance?

These topics are covered here, along with many others that show how breast cancer changes our bodies, abruptly shifts our careers, our relationships, our sense of ourselves in the world, but also how it makes us acutely aware of what we love, what we cling to, how we want to spend our precious moments on this earth. Despite everything, most of what we are living falls into the category of "not cancer" and the multifariousness of life pulls us along into so many things that we now experience with new eyes.

The title is drawn from a story, "The Day My Nipple Fell Off," by Laurie Hessen Pomeranz, which encapsulates it all with searing honesty: shock, mourning, humor, the surreal. If I told you that she lost her nipple twice (the same one), I'd already be revealing too much. The story centers this collection, which seeks to expose all the contradictory and messy emotions at once — the fear and the laughter, the grief and the gratitude.

The sense of loss that we all experience is so formidable and wears so many faces. We can't avoid it, and we don't want to. But woven around that, we live, and we live intensely. We love our partners, our kids, our parents; we learn to navigate the medical system and to push ourselves to new challenges; we befriend, we bemoan, and we heal. We also laugh at massively inappropriate things, like the surgery weight-loss plan and feeling each other up, but this is the laughter we need — to fend off the dark specters of anxiety and hopelessness and remind us that in this shitty club we found the most spectacular group of friends.

Solidarity is what it's finally all about. Being there for each other. In the hospital, the infusion center, the radiation waiting room. Fighting for insurance coverage and fighting for our lives. We visit each other. We hold each other. And we tell it like it is.

I. MEDICAL MAZE

Where's the Ma'am in Mammogram?

Dorinda Vassigh
May 2012

It's funny: I just now remembered being scared right before my mammogram. Strange, because ever since the diagnosis, I look back on that time as my "innocent" time, the time before the fear set in. I thought I didn't get scared until after the mammogram, when we sat in the room with the radiologist, and she started to point at my pictures and describe to Amanda and me (a less than enthused audience at that point) the specifics of the technology (picture her talking about how the machine works, or something of that ilk, while we're waiting to hear that I either do or do not have cancer). I remember the moment when I realized this could actually be real, I could actually have cancer.

The woman who administered the mammogram had a neurological problem, which made it difficult for her to steady my body in the "just-so" position that a procedure like this necessitates. She wobbled around and was so unsteady that she felt the need to tell me that she was not, in fact, drunk. I told her it never occurred to me that she was. I did *not* tell her that it did occur to me that she might be hopped up on methamphetamines. She couldn't get the picture quite right, and we had to keep redoing the test. Once... twice... After the second valiant attempt to squeeze me for all I was worth, Amanda dared me to tell her that "normally I get dinner first."

So, not wanting to back down from a dare, when the nurse told me to come in and redo the mammogram, I declared, "Normally, I make 'em buy me dinner first," and grinned a grin that I like to think must have surely communicated mischief. (On second thought, this is the same grin that I have been told by close friends and family to abandon.) I looked back at Amanda to see if she was laughing. She was, but the nurse was completely befuddled. I explained to her that she keeps making me undress, and doesn't even buy me a dinner first. "Get it?" I say, "Get it? Like it's a date!" She was nonplussed.

Nonetheless, the Vassigh sisters got a huge kick out of it. It's one of the few moments that I remember during that torturous process that made me smile and laugh, and, even for just a moment, reminded me that in this comedy of errors we call life, in the midst of our darkest days and our most fearful moments, we can find refuge in the camaraderie of an irreverent joke, a girlish giggle, a silly (or, depending on who is asked, ugly) grin. I took that little joke with me onto that weird contraption of a machine, and laid it right next to my body. I tried hard not to laugh on the third repeat of the test.

She got her fateful picture, and I got to put my shirt back on and go home—without dinner, without a sense of what the future holds, without even a "Thank you, ma'am."

Dr. Me

Ann Kim
May 2012

Shortly before my thirty-ninth birthday, when I was taking a shower, I felt a lump about the size and shape of a pea in my right breast. I felt a chill go through my body. A week later, on my birthday, I got a biopsy. When the doctor called with the results (I was setting out the birthday cake for my older son's seventh birthday), the news was bad: I had breast cancer. I wanted to cry, but I couldn't. It just felt surreal.

In literature and film, medicine is often depicted as a paternalistic profession, with patients given little information and expected to follow their doctor's orders blindly. In real life, my experience was the opposite. Instead of having an all-knowing doctor telling me what to do, I found myself with a team of doctors relying on me to make the critical treatment decisions. I was like a president with advisors, but I knew nothing about the topics, and the information and choices were overwhelming. What I expected was Dr. Brilliant Guide; what I got was Dr. Me.

My first appointment was with a preeminent breast surgeon at a top-rated comprehensive cancer center. She carefully laid out the options for me: lumpectomy with radiation or mastectomy with reconstruction. The lumpectomy would mean a less invasive procedure and a quicker recovery but also require several weeks of daily radiation and a lifetime of mammograms and MRIs. The mastectomy would entail more invasive surgery and a longer recovery time but eliminate the need for radiation and ongoing screening. Long-term survival odds were the same. My surgeon had no recommendation either way.

Anxious to get her to cast a vote, I tried a personal approach. I had Googled my surgeon before the appointment and found that we were of the same age and ethnicity, and we were both mothers. "You and I could be sisters—twins, even," I told her. "If you were in my shoes, what would you do?"

She paused before answering. "Whenever women ask me that, I tell them that it's a personal decision, and that I can't make it for them," she said. "But when I look at you, I see myself. I would choose a mastectomy with reconstruction."

I was grateful for her answer but also frustrated on behalf of other patients. Why do doctors express their much more informed opinion so reluctantly?

I had more decisions to make when I met with a plastic surgeon. He laid out the options: saline implant, TRAM flap (which uses skin, fat, and muscle from the belly region to construct a breast), or LAT flap (which uses skin, fat, and muscle from the back region to construct a breast).

Today, eight years later, with all the advances in reconstructive surgery, the possibilities (and acronyms) are even more numerous: DIEP, PAP, SGAP, I-GAP, SIEA, TUG, and ICAP flaps; the resurgence of the silicone implant; nipple-sparing surgery; and injection of liposuctioned fat.

These are probably improvements, but how well are most patients going to understand what they involve?

For my part, I chose to get an implant, but I developed severe capsular contracture, when scar tissue forms around the implant and causes painful stiffness and hardening of the tissue. After multiple surgeries, I had to remove the implant altogether. In retrospect, I wish I'd considered the choice of no reconstruction at all, but it was not something that I even thought to discuss with the plastic surgeon, nor did he mention it to me.

The hardest phase of my medical training was choosing an oncologist, the person responsible for administering chemotherapy and other systemic cancer treatments. Weeks had passed since my surgery, and I was convinced that the cancer was already beginning to spread. I wanted to begin chemotherapy right away. But the oncologist offered me the most intimidating set of choices yet.

I could take four rounds of Adriamycin plus Cytoxan, either at two-week or three-week intervals. I could add four rounds of Taxol or Taxotere, again at either two- or three-week intervals. I could participate in a clinical trial in which I would receive either a new drug called Herceptin or a placebo. After my chemotherapy ended, I could choose to take five years of an oral hormonal drug called Tamoxifen, or I could suppress my ovaries by taking a drug called Lupron or Zoladex and take five years of an Aromatase Inhibitor such as Letrozole (brand name Femara), Exemestane (Aromasin), or Anastrozole (Arimidex), or I could take five years of Tamoxifen and follow it up with another five years of an Aromatase Inhibitor.

My head was spinning. Having spent an hour describing the options, the oncologist had run out of time and had to move on to her next patient. Rather than recommending a particular course of treatment, the oncologist told me and my husband to go home and think about it and make an appointment to meet with her again.

I didn't want to wait several more weeks mulling over treatments I didn't really understand. At my friend's suggestion, I met with another oncologist. He offered the same options as the first oncologist but recommended a specific course of treatment and gave strong supporting reasons for it. I appreciated that he was advocating an aggressive approach (adding a third chemotherapy agent and combining ovarian suppression with an Aromatase Inhibitor). But, mostly, I was grateful for a straightforward answer. He became my oncologist.

For young women with breast cancer, treatment decisions often extend beyond surgery, radiation therapy, and oncology to medical specialties such as genetic counseling, fertility planning, gynecology, psychiatry, physical therapy, and primary medicine. Unfortunately, even at a comprehensive cancer center, the patient must coordinate these various disciplines. And if you go "a la carte" like I did, mixing and matching doctors in different practice groups and at different hospitals, good luck.

In the end, I had to create an Excel spreadsheet just to keep track of my appointments: breast surgeon every six months; mammogram every year (ideally just before the breast surgeon visit so that we could discuss the results); MRI every year for the first two years (ditto, but scheduled six months from the mammogram); oncologist every four months for the first five years, then every six months thereafter; ditto for the blood test with tumor markers; PET/CT every year for the first three years; bone density test every year for the first five years (to track the bone thinning effects of the Aromatase Inhibitors); MUGA heart scan every few months for the year of Herceptin (owing to the cardio-toxic effects of Herceptin and Adriamycin); gynecologist every six months; primary physician every year; and so on. I was able to keep track of this because I'm fairly organized. But what about most people?

In many respects, the collaborative approach that doctors take to cancer treatment is welcome. No one wants a high-handed doctor making treatment decisions without the patient's involvement or understanding. But a patient can't, in the end, play the role of doctor. We might want to know *why* a doctor is recommending something, but we still want a recommendation. Also, many of us need a guide just to navigate all the appointments and logistics, which can be byzantine.

Today, nearly eight years after my initial diagnosis, I continue to be vigilant in monitoring my health. (Hormone-sensitive cancers like mine have a "long tail"—meaning they can recur ten, fifteen, or even twenty years after diagnosis.) I read articles and books about cancer. I attend lectures and take notes about the latest treatments. And I participate in a breast-cancer support group.

If, knowing what I know now, I were able go back in time and advise myself, I would have said three things that I also say to new acquaintances in similar circumstances.

The first is that you should always bring a family member or friend to your appointments and have him or her take notes. Often, we patients are so overwhelmed that we can't remember what we were just told or don't ask any questions.

The second is that you must take care of your whole self. Treat yourself to delicious and healthful food every day. Watch a funny movie and laugh with your friends. Take naps and hot baths as needed.

The third is that you should feel free to complain. I have seen too many friends suffer in silence, whether the problem is nausea from chemo (doctors often prescribe the cheapest anti-nausea drugs before moving up to the more powerful stuff) or simply trouble getting an appointment. If the front desk or support staff are unhelpful, tell your doctor—doctors don't want to lose you as a patient.

In an ideal world, of course, no patient should have to shoulder so many responsibilities along with trying to get well. One of the best improvements that could be made would be for patients with cancer to have a "patient advocate."

If you were diagnosed with cancer, the medical center would partner you with a professional patient advocate who would guide you through the cancer treatment process. The patient advocate would set up appointments for you, make sure your care was coordinated, and offer general health-related suggestions (alternative treatments, massage, nutrition classes, support groups). The advocate might even accompany you to appointments and help you with decision making.

This would go a long way toward letting those with serious conditions have the luxury of being patients, so that they don't have to play Dr. Me.

Letter to My Left Breast

Erin Hyman
January 2012

Dear Left Breast,

So it's come to this. After all we've been through together, now you're trying to kill me? *Really*? Why couldn't you be more like your sister on the right? Loyal, patient, follows all the rules—you don't see her creating hot spots on the mammogram.

Haven't I been good to you? Don't you remember when I took that high-school job in that crappy bathing-suit shop just so I could get us bikinis that fit? (It *was* Palm Springs after all—we needed bikinis, even in February.) And what about college—junior year abroad was good: we went to Greece and stayed topless on the beaches for weeks. Never mind that ignoramus American boy who told me that I should do more push-ups so you would be perkier—the freedom! The lack of restraint! The warm Mediterranean water! It was heavenly for all of us.

OK, so pregnancy was a downturn, I'll give you that. You blew up to twice your size, and with the belly taking up so much real estate, there wasn't really any place to go. But don't you remember when I found the Belly Bra—a sea of Lycra to hold you, your sister *and* the belly in place—*that* was among the major engineering feats of our time!

And how could we have known then how much worse it would be when we got to breastfeeding? I mean, I hate to say it, but you doubled your bulk again. I think alone you were bigger than my head. But when you were engorged didn't I try everything to cool you off—cool gel doughnuts, cabbage leaves even? It was something of a shanda that The Pump Station in Santa Monica—a store entirely devoted to breastfeeding supplies—couldn't be bothered to carry a bra in our size. But hey, that's ancient history now!

Things returned to normal—well, mostly. So our bra size was a 32 long—we did downsize, after all! Fancy lingerie makers in far-off places finally woke up to our needs. People gave us compliments. All that exercise I did didn't really affect you, but hey it was good for the neighborhood! Collateral benefits, no? OK, so there was that one time I visited a plastic surgeon to talk about reducing you and your sister—it was a consultation only, nothing happened!

And now, after all this: mutiny. I have to get rid of you; I have no choice. How could I ever trust you again? And your sister? Well, guiltless she may be, but you took her down with you. Plus, I got a great deal on an upgrade—your replacements will stay aloft in even the most averse conditions. I get to realize my lifelong dream of going braless—even in public!

Sorry you won't be there to enjoy it with me.

Love,
Erin

The Count—324 Days Into This Mess

Nola Agha

1 mutated gene

1 breast removed

1 fainting episode

2 near-fainting episodes

2 days spent in the hospital post-surgery

3 surgeons—breast, plastic, and ob-gyn

4 cycles of dose-dense Adriamycin/Cytoxan

5 visits to the physical therapist

5 months of chemo

7 hours spent in surgery

7 positive lymph nodes

8 creams tested attempting to heal the radiation burn

9 scars

12 cycles of Taxol

13 visits to the lymphedema specialist

19 lymph nodes removed

27 daily pills (26 are vitamins and supplements)

27 radiation sessions

36 visits to the acupuncturist

63 sticks with a needle
90 minutes each day spent taking my homeopathic anti-cancer remedy
127 hospital gowns
165 people following my updates on CarePages
$9000+ raised for the Breast Cancer Fund
$661,536.06 cost of my treatment, to date

October 2011. My daughter's third birthday. The day of the Breast Cancer Fund's sixteenth-annual hike up Mt. Tam to raise money to prevent breast cancer. Just forty days after finishing my last round of radiation, I find myself in a dew-covered field at the base of Mt. Tam, where I meet a group of women from BAYS whom I have never met before but who know more about my current situation than most of my friends or family. In my back pocket is a list of names.

Up and up we hike. We pass through chaparral shrubs, fog-filled valleys, towering redwoods, moss-covered oaks. Mother Nature at her finest. It smells magnificent. Along the way, I talk with my teammates, all members of BAYS. We talk in cancer lingo along the way: "I was dx stage 1, May 2010, right mx, ACT, flap, now mets," says one. We discuss implants, surgeries, surgeons, and side effects, as only survivors can.

After passing through a tall, dark stand of redwoods, the trail curves tightly to the right to reveal the top. There are tents set up with food, water, and medical aid. After I consume the obligatory Gatorade and oranges, I climb to a rocky outcropping and pull out a tissue and the list of names from my back pocket. Looking in one direction towards the Pacific Ocean, with the frothy white waves crashing on Stinson Beach, and in the other towards the calm waters of the San Francisco Bay, I start to read the names. Hundreds of names. Names of every person who helped us along the way, offered a kind word, made us dinner, drove me to an appointment, wrote a card, called, posted a message, sent an email, took care of the kids, folded our laundry, sent flowers, took care of me, provided a flexible work environment, offered toys or books, washed our dishes, or otherwise made this whole nightmare easier and more tolerable. The strong wind carries the names from my lips towards God/Allah, Mother Nature, the universe, or whoever you want to believe is listening. Every one of these people carried me and lifted me up. Now, in return, I have carried them to the top of this mountain, where I send their names up in gratitude. I pull out another Kleenex, finish my list, and join my group as they head down the trail.

An hour and a half later, as we near the bottom, my legs are close to giving out. And just then, the leader of our group yells, "Nola! Look!" In his red-and-white-striped shirt and blue jeans, standing at a curve in the switch-backs, is my son, high up in my husband's arms, waving to the hundreds of women and men streaming down the trail. They are all laughing, smiling, waving, and as happy to see him as I am. My daughter is waiting at the bottom with my parents, holding a bouquet of yellow wildflowers. Fittingly, we finish the trail together, as a family.

324 days after beginning this adventure, I celebrate being alive and having the support of hundreds of friends and family across the globe, while shouting my thanksgiving from a mountain top.

Torture by Nursery Rhyme

Laurie Hessen Pomeranz
March 2012

Here we are, four days into my latest hospitalization. This breast infection situation is pretty crazy. I've spent eighteen of the last ninety days in the hospital, all to save a fake boob. I'm over it. Yesterday, the doctor talked me through the likelihood of having to lose the implant he put in three months ago. I've never seen anything like what I looked like yesterday. Think Dolly Parton. Now think, Dolly Parton *on fire*. Most of the day was spent in tears.

I was grateful, though, to enjoy two peaceful, tearful hours with my friend Kristin, who drove up from Santa Cruz to anoint me with rainwater, cover my body in flowers, sweep away bad energy, and cultivate healing by fanning me with a bundle of sage and an owl's wing, while she sang Native American songs to me and rubbed my feet with coconut butter. It was unlike anything I've ever experienced, and it was profoundly funky and totally cathartic. I love my friends and all the unique ways that people reach out in support.

This morning, my doctor and I were pleasantly surprised to see that the drugs seem to have finally kicked into action during the night. (Did the owl's wing do the trick?) The swelling has come down, significantly. Less Dolly, more Laurie. Less fire, more embers.

Yesterday, amidst my tears, grief, and panic over the thought of losing my breast (again), I entertained myself with gallows humor, imagining my future move to a cabin in Montana, next to Ted Kazcynski, the Uni-Bomber. I'd be Laurie Pomeranzski, the Uni-Boober. Hunkered away in isolation, I would write my Manifesto, or, in this case, my Manibreasto. That's not funny, that's sick—I realize. But that's how insane this feels sometimes.

I'm definitely feeling like Grandpa Joe and Grandma Josephine from *Willie Wonka and the Chocolate Factory*, who stayed in bed for years at a time. I'm ready to get up and click my heels and bust a move. One of the really sweet, funny residents came in the other morning and saw the crazy nest (fortress) that I've built here, which involves an inordinate amount of pillows on all sides of me. He said, "I understand we have a pillow shortage on the fifth floor, now I see why."

At least, it's comfy and bright in here. I have done nothing but lie in this bed for days, with two quick walks around the fifth floor (it's way too depressing out there, so I run back to my room). I have played five bajillion games of Words With Friends; I fear that if I am not released soon, my iPhone may actually fuse with the skin on my right hand. My room has an altar (it's a hospital shelf, but it makes a fine altar) full of flowers, Mardi-Gras beads, drawings from my friends' kids, my Stuart Hall wrestling T-shirt that says, "NEVER QUIT," my Giants sweatshirt, the jar of rainwater that Kristin painted me with, letters, cards, and a stuffed Micky Mouse holding a baseball bat.

A hospital floor is full of so many beeps and pings and moans and yelps, sounds of pain and suffering. Add to that the incessant parade of people coming in and out of the room with umpteen questions: Do I need spiritual care? How many times have I urinated in the last five hours? What percent of my breakfast did I eat? I wanted to yell, "LEAVE ME ALONE!" I told my nine-year-old son about the woman who came in to ask how many times I'd peed today, and Jack said, "Isn't that a little inappropriate?"

I snapped at one nurse's aide, "I'm sorry, but did you actually just wake me up to ask me how much of my breakfast I ate?" Don't they remember the old adage, "never wake a sleeping baby"? I am feeling like a baby at times— tearful, cranky, and wanting my mommy! Here I am in the infected aftermath of my cancer treatment, longing for my mom who never got to have an aftermath of her cancer treatment. God, she was brave.

Truly, the worst thing on this hospital floor is the "fall alarm." Because there are a lot of patients on this wing who are post-surgery, loopy in some way, and prone to falling, they have alarms on their beds. Every time a patient, such as my very squirrelly neighbor, tries to get out of bed (without a nurse there to support them), the fall alarm goes off. Guess what it does? It plays "Mary Had a Little Lamb"—and not the Jimi Hendrix version. The nursery-rhyme version. In this weirdo electronic piano riff. All day and all night, I'm hearing "Mary Had a Little Lamb." I'm ready to slaughter Mary and her flippin' lamb.

At 4:00 a.m., I called the nurse and told her that I was going to go off the deep end if I heard that song one more time. I asked her to knock me out with pain meds and Benedryl (fortunately, it was time for them anyway). She gave me the drugs, and some earplugs, and I got a couple of hours of sleep (until the Chaplain came in at 7:00 a.m. to see if I wanted "support with any of my spiritual traditions.") Are you *kidding* me? Go away! Or, at least, come back after they've loaded me up on hospital hash browns, and my husband, Jeff, has brought me a super-sized half-caff Starbucks. The only spiritual tradition I want support with at 7:00 in the morning is the ancient, deeply meaningful spiritual practice I like to call *sleep*. Can I get an "amen"?

An insane amount of action takes place outside, below my room. I am right above the garbage hauling area of the hospital. Regular garbage, bio-hazardous waste, recycling, linen deliveries, dishes and trays from the main hospital, all these come through the loading dock, right outside my window. And all of it involves dumpsters being emptied and a lot of trucks backing-up with beeping noises. Between these noises, the nurses' call bell (which rings anytime anyone needs something), IV alarms when medication bags are empty, and Mary, this is just a loud place to be. As I lay here trying to rest yesterday, amidst all the bells and beeps, I was envisioning the Will Farrell/Christopher Walken "More Cowbell" sketch on Saturday Night Live, changing the words to: "I've got a fever, and the only prescription is less call bell!" I laughed alone in my bed.

Jeff brought me a pint of Haagen-Dazs Rocky Road tonight, and I think I'll pop on a movie and eat the whole damn thing. That's how mama rolls when she's been in the same T-shirt for four days. Being hooked-up to ten feet of IV tubing means you can't shower, or even change your shirt. At least my hair is clean. Jeff came yesterday and washed my hair in the sink, and blew it dry. He even brought my yummy-smelling hair products from home. It was divine. The man is reaching new levels of sainthood every day. My favorite nurse and the front-desk clerk from the surgeon's office came to by to visit, and they arrived when Jeff was shampooing me. Upon seeing this, one of them said, "Oh...my...GOD. Do you have a brother?" Whoever says you can't meet a decent guy in a bar clearly has not met my husband.

It looks like I'll certainly be here through the week. My doc is well aware that come hell or high water, I intend to be on a plane to Arizona next Wednesday for our family trip to see the Giants in Spring Training. I'll be the crazy lady in the stands, screaming her lungs out, with a boob drain pinned to the inside of her Matt Cain T-shirt. Sexy.

Oh, there's Mary and her lamb again. Why do they have to play the *whole* song, *twice*? How about just a little beep or something? Or at least give us the Stevie Ray Vaughan version? I've complained about it to the nurses and they all say it makes them completely mental, too. Last night, I had another vision. I couldn't help thinking of that chilling scene in *Clockwork Orange* where the dude's eyes are held open with toothpicks and he's forced to watch a traumatic video. I felt similarly—like my ears were being held open and I had to endure this horrific, creepy, electronica nursery rhyme, over and over and over again. We should stop water-boarding detainees, and start playing this psycho nursery rhyme instead.

I'd tell anyone anything they wanted to know, if they'd just make it stop.

Story of Cancer-Land Young

Jennifer Mork

"I don't know how you lesbians feel about your breasts…"

"Well, Dad," I said, "we like them."

I could tell that my Dad was trying. That Christmas was full of blurry sadness. It was a low-key Christmas. I was hiding out on painkillers from the reality that I had cancer; going to expensive restaurants, receiving gifts of more bath products…as if the cancer could be fragranced. There was a drunken gaiety.

This was my before-chemotherapy talk, short and unemotional. "Are you ready?" he said. "Yes"—the "no" option was taken.

The call came during what I was told was the easy part: radiation. "Your dad has been in an accident. He is at Stanford."

I went to my third day of radiation and afterward drove my '86 Chevy Nova to Stanford. I asked the Stanford people where the emergency hospital was. They referred me to the cancer center. I was still bald.

It was going to be that kind of lifetime.

My Dad's family was gathering and I was their secret malady of imperfection. Cancer is the women's family curse. Reproductive cancers—we are chock full. Everyone said how good I looked; I didn't scare them with my outward frailty.

I went back and forth to Stanford all that month in nice cushy cars. My aunts were driving, telling me stories of my Dad and Grandmother.

My Dad's brain was disorganized and split wide open. He could only talk, not comprehend, as that is a function of memory, something he kept forgetting to have. We had the conversations about dying we could never have before.

"Jenni," he said, in a little-boy voice. "I don't want to die. Do you think I am going to die?"

"I don't know, Dad. Everyone is doing what they can." He wanted a priest. I catered to whims.

He always recognized my brother and me. He never forgot to ask how I was doing, my baldness being a visual cue to my present state.

He told other doctors, "I trust her judgment"—a phrase I never heard when his mind was guarded by a skull. Before his accident, he was always trying to leave. But now, I found that his core self was earnest and well meaning in every intention. "Ok, Jenni," he said, "get me my pants and a cup of coffee."

The days in the hospital were filled with fanciful conversations. The reality of my current life was far less than fanciful, and he couldn't remember anything for more than two minutes. The realm of fantasy proved a meeting ground. While visiting on Father's Day, my Dad acted as his doctor, diagnosing people on *Law and Order* and ordering them medical workups.

I saw how vulnerable he was, and how the identity of a person could be forever altered on the indent of a road.

The nights of sliding terror, of being trapped in a body that one day might self-devour. My Dad's body being able, but his mind chaotic and slippery. Recovery for each of us uncertain, as the outcome of each is never guaranteed. His accident and my cancer could not be construed as anything but drawing a bad hand.

I would sit waiting for radiation with nowhere to hide in my mind. I was cold in the cloth gown everyday. The machine whirring above me. I would think, "If only I could only go back to just having cancer today." The tension of my big life bulging.

Time kept happening: 12, 14, 17, 21 radiation sessions. My Dad transitioned to different levels within Stanford and then to rehab hospital. My skin raw, red, stinging, burning. I am growing fuzz believing it to be hair. It came in a fashionably shocking white.

My Dad started recounting information that was actually relevant. He said that he remembered what I wore when he first started remembering: a long polka-dotted skirt. I knew that my non-compliance in the khaki code of conduct was meaningful. My badge of fierce femme-ness was shiny and outremembered all beige.

Planning is a luxury that cancer never accommodates. I finished my radiation on July 7th, my Dad's birthday. The same day he was released from the hospital to be at home for his birthday. We celebrated together in his house. I—a fuzzy-headed, two-breasted self—went to the house where I spent my teenage years. My dad was talkative, emotive, impulsive, and alive. We had both made it through, but no longer in the homes of the selves that we resided in before.

I learned that we are nothing but the present. Wearing helmets and eating all your vegetables is not a safeguard of a known future. And acknowledging death makes living the hard edge of joy.

II. BODY BLOWS

The Day My Nipple Fell Off

Laurie Hessen Pomeranz
November 2012

So many bizarre, unexpected, and undignified things happen once one hops on-board one of the crappiest rides in the Amusement Park of Life: The Cancer Roller Coaster! It will make you scream, want to puke, turn you upside down, and if you're very lucky, land you back to somewhere close to where you started, feeling jostled and lucky to have survived.

When my (total babe of a) surgeon explained that my mastectomy would be "skin and nipple sparing," I thought I'd hit the jackpot on breast cancer. I wouldn't have one of those brutal-looking diagonal scars across the chest where the breast once was, leaving a large, tender gash in its place.

He would remove the tumorous breast by opening it from the underside, lifting it up, and scooping everything out. I imagined it like a big melon-balling operation. Keeping my skin and nipple intact, he would burrow under my pectoral muscle, and put in a tissue expander. In my mind, I thought of all the chickens whose breast skin I'd lifted to stuff with herb butter. I tried to console myself with this thought, as if he was just tucking some herb butter under my skin, not pulling up my pectoral muscles and shoving in an industrial-grade plastic bag, which he would inject with blue saline every week until I was filled like a balloon about to pop.

My plastic surgeon and his lively, fabulous Nurse Practitioner would stretch my pectoral muscles over many months. Once the space—one not meant to have anything under it—was stretched enough, there would be room for a lovely, squishy silicone sphere to eventually be placed in its stead. As the *pièce de resistance*, when he put in the implant, he would also lift and reduce my other breast, for a nice matching pair. Bam: a new, hot rack! (Although I'd always loved my rack before, I had to admit that the aesthetics had taken a beating since motherhood.) The new boobs would be my consolation prize for breast cancer, and the antidote to post-nursing droopers. ("Ptotic" is the medical term for droopy boobs. Did you know that?) It was rather depressing when my plastic surgeon referred to my "ptotic breasts," but I tried to appreciate the silver lining of learning a new vocab word.

What I never expected is that my nipple-sparing mastectomy would not, in fact, spare my nipple, and that I'd become one of the small percentage of women who experience nipple necrosis after a mastectomy. Nipple necrosis. DEAD NIPPLE. Shrivelly, dead, dried-up old nipple. No blood flow. Connection to circulation: severed. The nipple withers on the vine like forgotten grapes, like the stump on a baby's umbilical cord, and falls off.

After my surgery, my nipple was swaddled in gauze and balms to help it heal. It was normal that it looked traumatized, I'd just had a mastectomy, after all. However, at a post-op appointment a month or so after surgery, my nurse was concerned that the healing wasn't happening, and things were going in a downhill direction for my nipple. (Although my nipple was no longer *pointing* downhill.)

We decided that I'd keep my traumatized little eraser nub wrapped and protected, while we waited to see if the blood flow returned. Things weren't looking hopeful, though, as my nipple went from a high beam to something that looked more like an old mosquito-bite scab. My nipple was deflating and dying with each passing day, until it finally became clear that it would not miraculously rejuvenate.

The only thing left to do was just wait for it to fall off. The mere thought of my nipple drying up and falling off had me in a state of pretraumatic stress. I was a wreck. I imagined how much it would hurt when it finally came off, and how metaphoric and heart-breaking it felt that the very nipple that had fed and nourished my son, from my abundantly milky left breast, was dying.

For three full months, I wore a gauze patch inside my bra, protecting my vulnerable, crusty nipple from snagging and ripping off. I was desperately trying to postpone the inevitable. I believed that somehow, if I just kept my nipple protected, it wouldn't jump ship.

One day during this bizarre and emotional time, as I catastrophized about my impending loss, my seven-year-old son came home from his after-school program with a burning question.

"What does 'motherfucker' mean?" Jack asked, with his head cocked in curiosity.

"Oh, wow, that's a really bad put-down, Jack. You would never want to call someone that, it's a very mean word. Where did you hear it?" I asked, in my most innocuous Colombo-tone, trying to conceal my mortification.

"I heard it in after-care today. Some of the kids were having a swearing contest." He paused; I could tell his mind was hard at work on something. "How come no one says 'fatherfucker'?"

I couldn't muster anything better than, "That's a great question, buddy." He drifted off into distraction, and I went to my room and sobbed.

My tiny baby, who had nuzzled against my now vanished breast, who had drunk from the faucet of my now withering nipple, was growing up and hearing swear words, and beginning to contemplate what (the fuck) a fatherfucker would be. It was just too much, too soon, my baby becoming a teenager, a man, his old, cancerous mother no longer needed to feed and nourish him. The nipple became a symbol of the death of innocence, of the severing of the mother-child connection, as I began torturing myself with the inevitability of my child leaving home one day. Sure, that day was at least eleven years away, but I experienced the pain of it as if it was happening that very night right after dessert. My necrotic nipple was making me a neurotic cripple. I had to flop out on my bed and just howl with grief.

At my next doctor's appointment, my nurse delivered the unfortunate news that there was simply no way that my nipple was going to recover, and that I needed to start *leaving it uncovered* when I slept, so it would dry-up completely and fall off. I tortured myself with thoughts of my nipple snagging on my blanket, or my jammies, and ripping off. I thought of the waves of pain that would grip me when it happened. I needed sleeping pills to knock myself out and be able to rest. I slept in the softest T-shirt I have, the one with holes that I've been wearing since high school. I continued to cover my nipple with gauze by day, to protect it from friction in my bra.

One morning, maybe a week into the sleeping-without-gauze routine, I woke up and started to get dressed. When I got ready to put on my bra, I looked down and saw that my nipple was gone. Gone. It had fallen off in my sleep.

Frantically, I searched the bed (not sure what I thought I'd do when I found it). It wasn't on the sheets. It wasn't stuck to the inside of my T-shirt. I combed the carpet (which is rather scab-colored, now that I think of it) and the nipple was nowhere to be found. It had vanished. I hurled blankets every which way, to no avail. My left nipple was M.I.A.

On the one hand, I was hugely relieved that there was no pain, and in fact that the dreaded event had passed without so much as a wrinkle in my sleep. On the other, I was utterly mystified that my nipple had gone missing.

Dressed and ready for the day, I headed out. While we were all gone, to work, and school, and chemotherapy, our cleaning woman came for her monthly visit. Coming home to a clean house and a freshly-made bed was a real treat, until it dawned on me that my nipple had probably gone through the washing machine with the sheets, or taken up residence in our vacuum bag. Things turned from terrifying to comic for me with this realization. I'm thinking there aren't many housekeepers who have vacuumed up their clients' nipples.

When Jack was a baby and his umbilical cord stump dried up and fell off, I kept it. It sat on my nightstand, that little crusty stump of hard, desiccated tissue. I was attached to it, because it was the last fleshy fragment of what had connected my son and me to each other. I wasn't ready to let it go.

One day, however, when I headed off with the baby for the day, that same monthly housekeeper came. She cleaned all the surfaces, including my nightstand, and *threw away the stump*. I came home, and it was gone. The newly uncluttered, well-dusted nightstand was lovely, but Jack's umbilical cord stump was gone. When a friend from high school came over later that night, to meet my baby for the first time, I told her what had happened. She wasn't a mom yet, and said, "Ewww! You were *keeping* it? That's *sick*, my friend." Not sure what I thought I'd do with that old stump, or with that old nipple, but somehow I didn't want them to just go out with the trash. Compost, at least?

This body of mine has been through hell and back on the cancer ride. My breast was removed, my nipple died and fell off, and my areola peeled off with radiation. I had a bald head from chemo, and a bald boob, too. Like a moonscape, without the craters. Far from it, it was stretched out and overexpanded with saline to get me all plump and ready for the silicone. I look at photos now of my bulging naked breast, and it looks like I was smuggling a bowling ball under my pectoral wall.

Last Christmas, I went in to get my silicone implant and my reduction and lift. All I wanted for Christmas were my two front teats! It was not to be, however. A series of complications, infections, and the lingering trauma of radiation left me unable to heal. After three hospitalizations and eighteen days spent as an inpatient, the breast implant had to come out. Now, rather than a smooth moonscape full of saline, I have what looks more like the site of a bomb blast. A deep crater remains, where my breast once was, where my implant once filled in as a proxy. All that is left is the skin from that fallaciously named skin- and nipple-sparing mastectomy. That spared skin now adheres to my chest wall in a wrinkly mess that looks more like an elephant ankle than I care to admit, in a deep concavity that used to be my beautiful breast.

I'm two years out from cancer treatment now, and the side effect that most lingers (aside from the indignities of medically induced menopause, chemo brain, and aching joints from anti-estrogen treatments) is the pain from the year of pectoral trauma.

Herb butter would have been much gentler.

My New Weight-Loss Plan

Nola Agha

For the past week, since my DIEP-flap reconstruction, I've been alpha-testing a new weight-loss plan.

Start by scheduling a complex surgery that will require cutting big chunks of fat from your stomach and fashioning them into a breast. Post-surgery recovery requires an ICU stay and lots of physical immobility. As the date approaches, your stress will increase as you watch your kids, husband, family, and friends become increasingly worried about you. Stress is great for burning calories. Check into hospital as stress is peaking and sleep blissfully for about nine hours.

When you wake, you'll be in the ICU, attached to well over twenty tubes, wires, and monitors. No food or drinks allowed! Only an IV drip. This is great for weight loss. Spend the next few days sweating out extra fluid. Pain serves as additional appetite suppressant.

By the second day, transition to a liquid diet. Water, broth, juice, and jello continue the whole body cleanse. Listen carefully for innumerable "code-blue" and "rapid-response teams" being sent to nearby rooms to try to resuscitate sick patients. While this is a frank reminder of the fleeting nature of each human life, it more effectively serves as motivation to eat healthy and exercise every single day once out of the hospital.

Continue to breathe deeply every hour to remove fluid from lungs and reduce the chance of pneumonia.

Slowly remove wires, tubes, and monitors as strength resumes. Begin exercise regimen. Start small: attempt to get out of bed, walk two steps to chair, and sit. Two nurses necessary to assist. Try not to faint. Over the next few days, continue this exciting exercise regimen.

Transition to mushy foods: applesauce, mashed potatoes, soup that is thicker than clear broth. Continue getting out of bed to chair with assistance. Start taking more steps.

Be sure to take antibiotics during the surgery that will lead to eventual diarrhea. This appears to be the key to maintaining weight loss once resuming solid foods. Switch antibiotics to get rid of infection caused by first antibiotic.

After six long days in the hospital, go outside, breathe fresh air, and sit in the warm sunshine. Go home, see children, and become energized by the power of a thousand colliding suns. Shuffle around the house. Cats will automatically warm your feet and snuggle with you in bed to help improve endorphin flow.

The final step appears, thus far, to be the most controversial. First, create conditions that are equivalent to running on grass—uneven surfaces use more stabilizing muscles. Set 2.9 earthquake to go off at 5:30 a.m. Wake up. Sleepy husband will ask if it's thunder. Immediately after, cue a jolting 4.0 earthquake and a simultaneous crying child. Jump out of bed using stomach muscles and two arms that are *not* supposed to be used for jumping out of bed. See if you survive. Ingest major pain meds.

Thus far, the alpha test shows that the weight loss is real. The destabilizing muscle test seems to be way too early to perform on Day 7. Self-induced diarrhea may be too much to ask of some patients, although unexpected infection has added benefits in weight loss as well as improved mobility from frequent trips to the bathroom.

Alpha-test to continue for the next few weeks.

These Effin' Drains

Erin Hyman
January 2012

Sung as a Country-Western ditty (cowboy hat optional):

I'd be tellin' no lie,
committin' no perjury,
if I declare these things
worse than the surgery.

As if it weren't bad enough
not to have a boob there,
now I've got two plastic bulbs
hangin' by a tube there.

Chorus:
Don't mean to complain,
but these effin' drains
are driving me insane!

Two on each side—
couldn't it have been one?
Draining your chest fluids
really ain't no fun!

Two on each side,
fillin' up with your juices.
If my chest were a poker hand,
I'd be holdin' all deuces.

And they give you a camisole
to cover up the trauma,
but it just gives you the silhouette
of a suicide bomber...

Don't mean to complain,
but these effin' drains
are driving me insane!

I got back from the hospital
to find troubles with the pipes.
Toilet, sink, and washing machine —
we got a whole mess of gripes.

Then to add to my woes,
after the hideous operation,
the drugs they give for pain
make for world-record constipation.

So it seems nothing round here
has working pipin'...
except for these effin' drains
so I oughta quit my gripin'.

Meeting Las Vegas

Dorinda Vassigh
December 2012

I ended up in the basement of a McMenamins Hotel. This particular hotel's theme was musicians, rock and roll, and the rock-and-roll lifestyle. I found myself having a drink in the basement listening to a band—it felt almost as if life hadn't changed that much. I could still enjoy the sheer pleasure I derive from having a cocktail in a moldy, smelly little venue, listening to live music.

As I was getting ready to go back to my hotel, the singer started talking about his favorite stripper. (Portland has the highest per capita strip joints in the country, and good or bad, people just seem to have a much more relaxed approach to the sex industry in general.) He mentioned that this stripper, Viva Las Vegas, was a writer and an artist, and that she had written the most profound account he has ever read on the health industry, breast cancer, and her mastectomy.

When I got back to the hotel, I scoured the Internet to stalk her proper. I read the articles that the musician spoke of, but that wasn't enough. I realized I needed to meet her. I needed to meet someone who had one breast taken, and who still had the confidence to take her shirt off in front of a roomful of complete strangers.

As it turns out, she was performing at one of the oldest strip joints in Portland the following day from 4:00 to 10:00 p.m. I cancelled my prepaid nighttime tour of the underground tunnels.

I called my new friend Tom, who I had just met a few days prior, and asked him to come with me. I couldn't imagine going into a strip club alone. Never, in my wildest dreams, did I think that I would ever pick up a phone and ask a man that I barely knew to come with me to a strip joint to find a woman and get her to talk to me about her boobs. I told Tom I wanted to get there early, because getting there after the sun goes down seems seedy somehow.

So I got there at 4:00. Tom didn't. I waited for him for a bit outside the club, but the guys who passed by me on the street were looking at me funny. I got self-conscious and wondered if they thought I was some kind of a stripper stalker, or perhaps they thought I was trying to find a job. And if they were, were they laughing at me for being so presumptuous? Were they thinking to themselves, "Oh, honey, you are *not* stripper material. You need to drop about twenty pounds and maybe a couple of years..." I decided to just go inside the club. Surely, it couldn't be worse than loitering outside of it.

I stepped in, took a peek. The woman on the stage immediately saw me, pointed at me, and motioned me to come inside. So I did what any one of you in the same situation would do. Look at her, take it completely in... actually, she's not much skinnier than me, or much younger—so there, all you mean-spirited people in my imagination. There.

Then, I bolted. I ran back outside and called the friend who had introduced me to Tom, the guy who still hadn't shown up. I asked her if he was a flake. She said no. So I waited. It seemed like hours, but was probably just a few minutes.

Tom showed up. We went inside together and sat down. When the older woman behind the bar came to ask us what we wanted to drink, we gave her our orders. She sighed and said something like, "Well, I guess I'm a cocktail waitress now…" Tom thought we were supposed to go to the bar and get our drinks before sitting down.

The chairs in the bar were all facing the stage. Seated was a man, his wife, and his friend. A beautiful blond woman was on stage. She was wearing a tiny white cashmere sweater that barely came down to her midriff, panties, and heels. She seemed somewhat disinterested, dancing while talking to the bartender/cocktail waitress. Tom said he thought she was Viva Las Vegas. I said no way. Viva Las Vegas is going to be dressed up with glitter and feathers and big hair (hey, I live in San Francisco and hang out with drag queens – what do you expect?) This woman's schtick seemed to be more schoolgirl naughty than over-the-top glam.

Tom went to the bar and asked the bartender when Viva Las Vegas was going to dance. He said that his friend—and he pointed in my direction—came here just to see her, and explained how I'd read her articles online and I really wanted to meet her and maybe talk to her for a second. The bartender pointed at the naughty-schoolgirl dancer and said, "that's her, and she's fabulous."

She finished her set and walked towards me and shook my hand. I told her that I had read about her and read her article in *The New York Times*, detailing her experiences with breast cancer, and her boyfriend, and her band. She asked me, "Oh, are you in the industry?" I was flattered, and flustered, and laughed awkwardly.

Tom explained to her what we were doing there and she seemed, of all things, touched! I think she was happy that we were there to talk to her about her writing and her experiences, not just stare at her (though truthfully, I did do a little staring).

She was adorable, and sweet, and, best of all, open to answering all my questions. And I had a lot. I had read a lot about her the night before, and I knew that she had dated a mortgage broker after she was diagnosed. I asked her if she was still dating him. She said no. I also read that she had tried to do a "Run for the Cure" fundraiser during chemo and that on the way she and her friends popped into a bar and decided to just stay there all day instead of run. They started a tradition called "Drink for the Cure." I had also read details of her mastectomy and wanted to clarify some questions on reconstruction, and she answered all of them graciously—although possibly slightly creeped out that I knew so much about her life. I figured she's used to way more creepiness than what I'm giving her.

Eventually, she had to start back to work. Tom and I both sat at the stage to watch her, and the three of us continued our conversation. When you sit at the stage like that, the etiquette is to tip one dollar per song, so each new song that came on, we took out a dollar. We continued putting dollar bills on the stage and talking to her as she slowly shuffled out of garments, one at a time.

The conversation went something like this:

"So, did you have radiation?"

"No, see—they're both the same color," and she took off her shirt. The guys behind us start applauding. I scoot up closer to get a good look.

"Wow! Looks fantastic! Totally even."

"Yeah, I had a good surgeon." And she spanks herself and gets more applause.

"So, you had a nipple-sparing mastectomy right?"

"Yep, you know way too much about me," and she laughs.

"But, you still can't feel anything right?"

"Not much. See?" She pinches her nipple and the guys love it. We carry on like this for a while—me asking questions, her answering them while slowly taking more and more garments off, no one seeming to mind that she's multitasking.

I look behind me and see that the other woman in the audience looks a little uncomfortable and I smile at her. She smiles back. The husband says to her, "See, it's no biggie. You can go sit at the stage and tip a dollar or two. She's doing it."

I answer, "Oh, I put on a good show, but I don't feel completely comfortable either," and I smile at the woman again. He looks at me as if I've stabbed him in the back.

I tell Viva Las Vegas that I'd like her to sign my copy of her book, and also, that I'd like to first buy her book—does she have copies here at the bar? She does. She tells the bartender that I'm going to purchase her book and then continues dancing. The bartender now loves me and Tom, because we love Viva Las Vegas. She disappears for a moment and comes out with the book, *Magic Gardens*, and, as she hands it to me, tells me that it's a great book, and that I'll love it, and that Viva Las Vegas is brilliant and she's not *just* a stripper—she's a writer. I make a joke about how she should be Viva's literary agent.

When the set ends, she puts on her robe and comes to sit with us. I ask her how she found the courage, after having had her surgery, to get back on stage and show her breasts, one real and one fake. How did it feel the first time? She says the first few times back on stage she was terribly scared, but it got easier and easier.

Viva signs my book and in it she writes, "Thanks for making my day!"

I started getting ready to leave, finished my beer, and donned my coat. I knew there were probably rules about not touching the strippers, but I wanted to give her a hug.

I was about to leave when she exclaimed, "Oh, give me a hug!" She hugged me and gave me her email address.

I've since kept in touch with her, writing her emails and urging her to write her next book. In her latest email to me, she wrote:

> *I do still struggle with accepting my new breasts . . . they do seem quite a bit different to me; but life is change, and our bodies tell our stories one way or another. I like to think that I'd still strip if I had no nipples or even no reconstruction. Perhaps I'd even prefer that–having bits of plastic in my chest feels rather insincere. Acceptance, acceptance, acceptance...*

I was supposed to have the first part of my reconstructive surgery a few weeks ago. My surgeon was to switch out my expander—the temporary device that is currently lodged in my chest—for the silicone. I cancelled the surgery. I chickened out—at least, that's what I've been telling people, that I'm scared of surgery, that I don't want to deal with the drains, that I'm enjoying life, and I don't want it to be interrupted by yet another surgery.

But the truth is, I'm scared. Sometimes, I worry that my future body will give me cancer again, but I'm constantly worried that my future body will look ugly. I know that right now, naked, I look odd, lopsided, disfigured. But that's how I'm supposed to look while in between real implant and expander. On some level, I've come to terms with both the physical inconvenience and discomfort of the expander. I derive psychological comfort from knowing that while it looks weird, it's not my body that looks like that, it's this temporary piece of metal and plastic that is not part of my body, that doesn't really belong in me and because of that, I can feel that *it* looks this way, not that *I* look this way. I haven't yet come to terms with the future, and with the knowledge that this man-made new body part won't be the same as the sensate one that God made. So I'm staying in this strange "in-between body" for a little longer, and hopefully, by the time my next scheduled surgery date rolls around, I will have learned "acceptance, acceptance, acceptance..."

How We Wound Up Topless

Laurie Hessen Pomeranz
December 2010

A few nights ago, I felt up five women.

I'm a happily married forty-two-year-old woman with an eight-year-old son. So how did I end up inside the bathroom of a downtown brew pub with my face in all those knockers, the bare breasts of a group of women I'd just met, with our shirts up and bras hoisted? All the stroking and pressing and gazing might sound like fodder for *Penthouse* forum.

Actually, we're all breast-cancer patients and survivors.

Last summer, I had a mastectomy. I finished chemotherapy two weeks ago. December and the beginning of the new year will be filled with holiday celebrations—and daily radiation. Currently, my left breast is stuffed with a rigid, plastic, saline-filled chest-expander, a space holder for my future silicone implant. The surgical swap-out will happen next summer, after radiation is completed, and my skin has healed for the requisite six months.

How I long for a breast with a little softness and droop to it! How I look forward to having a breast that you'd want to have some fun with, not something you try not to bonk into.

I don't exactly love having one perky, overly firm, scarred, bolt-upright breast and one natural, low-slung, post-nursing breast that I can practically tuck into my jeans. But I'll take these mismatched breasts any day. I'm alive, and I'm thankful.

On Wednesday, I'm at a cocktail hour organized for local young women coping with breast cancer. I like being around women who know what this is like. We speak in shorthand. We cut to the chase. That night, we talk openly about each others' diagnoses and healthcare providers, we compare notes on our chemo days, what we wore on our bald heads, how breast cancer has affected our relationships and decisions around childbearing.

We also talk about surgery scars, radiation burns, creams and potions to help repair the damage. We commiserate over the lack of sensation in our reconstructed breasts and nipples, about losing our eyelashes, about setting limits with our loved ones who are scared. The conversation flows steadily, energetically, as we sip beer, pear cocktails, and sangria, and eat fried potatoes with brava sauce. Along the way, the topic turns to nipple tattoos.

A nipple tattoo involves inking a fake nipple onto a post-mastectomy breast, if the nipple was not spared, or if, as in my case, it did not survive surgery. I'm very curious about nipple tattooing, so I begin to ask questions. How do they reconstruct a nipple? How well do the areola and nipple color match the healthy breast, if one still remains? One of the women offers to show me her nipple tattoos before we all head home. Sounds great.

Ten o'clock rolls around, and it is time for people to call it a night. Breast-cancer patients and survivors try to practice moderation with regard to alcohol, though sometimes with more success than others. Alcohol can elevate estrogen production, which may lead to tumor growth or recurrence in those of us with estrogen-sensitive tumors. So tonight's crew has enjoyed two or three drinks apiece, though certainly we all would love to toss back a few more. We are the pictures of moderation and restraint.

The check is paid, the beautiful woman with the nipple tattoo says, "Let's go to the bathroom, and I'll show you my boobs." The other women all want to see them, too. No fools in this crowd. Plus, some have to pee. So off we all go: The divine secrets of the ta-ta sisterhood.

With all of us clustered together by the sinks, the woman yanks up her top and pulls down her bra. We all take in her perfect, enviable cleavage, and her tattooed areola and nipple. She offers to let us touch her reconstructed breast. I'm thrilled. Though I've had a lap dance, I've never actually laid my hands on a silicone implant. I'm dying to know what it will feel like. I'll soon have my own.

Quickly, the rest of us want to show and tell and cop a feel. Shirts are raised, bras lowered, and fingers, hands, and eyes begin moving all over the smooth, the scarred, the lumpy, storied terrain of twelve breasts. The chatter is constant. You know how we girls are when we get in a bathroom together.

Just outside the restroom door, in a private party room, a reunion is in progress. The Class of '82 from a posh New England boarding school is busy reacquainting itself. What do those post-preps think as they come in to use the bathroom and find six women baring their racks? The contrast between "us" and "them" feels striking. Then again, considering that one in eight women are diagnosed with breast cancer, chances are a few of those unintentional interlopers have stories of their own.

Though I have only just met my comrades in cancer, we feel safe with each other. We are young, vital women, who look in the mirror and see purple scars and disfigurement, in addition to vibrancy and bravery. We know what it feels like to wonder how our partners or prospective partners see us when our tops are off. And in a culture obsessed with perfect jugs, we understand being grateful for whatever was spared — or can be rebuilt.

Look Good...Feel a Whole Lot Better!

Sarah De Haaff
November 2011

I just finished reading a book called *Why I Wore Lipstick to my Mastectomy* and while I get the premise—lipstick as a symbol of femininity, power, and even control in a chaotic and helpless situation—it was a little heavy on the lipstick references. For my taste, anyway...I kept getting distracted. *But maybe it's because I don't wear lipstick that often.*

It got me thinking. Vanity is sneaky. It kind of exists, low profile, without demanding much attention until something happens to jeopardize your appearance. Then you realize that vanity was right there with you all along.

Vanity *can* be a good thing. It's that healthy motivation to shower or brush your hair in the morning or wear something other than sweatpants everyday. It's the thing that inspires us to put our best foot forward, our best self out there in the world, or at least what we think of as our best self.

It's why sometimes, when I'm feeling really crappy, just taking a shower and getting dressed can make me feel better even though nothing has really changed.

We all have different levels of caring what others think of

us. But we care.

While reading the book, I definitely related to the emotional aspects of losing one's hair and feeling less feminine; it *is* quite a shock. Still, the author goes on and on lamenting changes in physical appearance and I kept thinking they probably could have been covered in a chapter or two. Not a whole book.

The American Cancer Society, in partnership with a few other agencies, created a program called "Look Good, Feel Better." It is designed to help women cope with the emotional aspects of going through cancer treatment and all of the side effects. Different companies and agencies donate beauty products for free makeup kits. They have workshops and events all over, and it's all free to cancer patients. The workshops cover everything from wigs, to makeup, to skincare, during and after treatment.

It is amazing to realize how much looking "like oneself" matters.

Some days, I look in the mirror and don't recognize myself. This is psychologically and emotionally disorienting. The mental picture I have of how I look is based on thirty-seven years of data. These last few months, while dramatic, are short in comparison to the many years I have looked like myself. The new data does not compute and continues to catch me off guard.

So, the effort I used to put into looking "*good*" now goes into looking "*normal*." The object is passing as a regular person, not necessarily standing out. Don't get me wrong, I wear wigs and makeup for the sake of my own psyche, but also so that I don't have to talk about it all the time to strangers. Or get sympathetic looks from people on the street.

I have not yet fully embraced the bald look. I am getting there, but have yet to really rock it out in the real world. I do it at home, but we've started to notice that my kids are a little more clingy and cranky when I do. So I try to look normal for them too. Plus, now it's getting colder and I seem to need a hat all the time. Apparently, all that hair really did serve a purpose!

Rarely do I go out of the house without makeup on these days. Mostly for me, but also because I am trying not to scare people. Unfortunately, the way that the social worker told me about the "Look Good, Feel Better" program was not especially inspiring. She said something about how I would *finally* learn how to apply makeup.

Wait...What are you saying? I am sitting here in front of you, fully made up, and you are telling me that I need to go somewhere to learn how to do it correctly?

Are you telling me that all of my years of hanging out with girlfriends, trading beauty secrets, poring over fashion magazines, endless high-school camp-outs in the beauty-products aisles at drug stores, and all of our makeup sessions at various cosmetic counters have done nothing?

That's kinda rude. And not really taking a pulse of the situation and gearing your presentation toward the person sitting in front of you. Not that I am a makeup expert, but *come on*, I think I'm pulling it off. No one has ever told me to go fix my face or tried to wipe my makeup off. Well, not since I was thirteen, anyway.

"No, no," she says, "I just meant that *some* women tell me that they got so much out of it because they finally learned how to put on makeup after all these years..."

OK. That's great. Super. Look, all I really want to know is how to draw on eyebrows when they are gone.

Because I've never actually had to do that before. And I may have slept through that part of my extensive makeup training. My eyebrow history has only included removal of some extraneous hairs. Thanks to some strong super-duperhairy genes, my sisters, cousins, and I have always battled the bushy-eyebrow war. Sometimes more successfully than others. And I think I can speak for all of us when I say that we are just pretty darn grateful that eyebrows are back "in."

So despite the fabulous sell job the social worker did for this "Look Good, Feel Better" event, I didn't end up going. Maybe some other time, but for now, I figure that since I don't need any more wigs, and I have plenty of makeup, I can do my own penciling-in-eyebrow research and save myself the trip.

Make no mistake, vanity aside, it makes a huge difference in my perspective and outlook when I tend to my appearance. I remember being on maternity leave and forcing myself to shower and put on regular-people clothes most days because it made such a difference. The same is true during this process. Even though I am exhausted, the effort pays off. If I look sick, I feel worse. Something about the outside matching the inside. People keep saying, "you look great!" which also helps. I can't help thinking they sound a tiny bit surprised.

Underneath all the "stuff," I am a bald, pale, tired-ass chemo patient. But that's where makeup and wigs come in. When I gather up all of my little assistants and overdo it, I am even able to pass for "normal." Sometimes, I feel like I should have a big awards show and thank all my assistants.

I'd like to thank...

* LAURA MERCIER TINTED MOISTURIZER: for making me look a little more human and a little less ghost-like.

* BENEFIT POSIE TINT: for bringing color back to my life...or face. (Grey is not really my color.) You are truly a miracle worker and kind of my best friend right now.

* BRONZER: for making it look like I actually get outside.

*MASCARA/LIQUID LINER: for helping to create the illusion that I have more than ten lashes left, and thus preventing my eyes from fading into the rest of my face. Who knew that eyelashes made such a dramatic difference in one's appearance? (I may have to consider switching to waterproof, as Taxol is making my eyes water all the time.)

*LIPGLOSS or CHAPSTICK: for nurturing my freakishly dry lips.

*LOTION: For literally being there for me morning, noon, and night. No matter how much I slather on, my skin is always thirsty for more!

And of course I want to acknowledge my fabulous wigs: LUCY, MIRANDA, JOY, NOEL, CLAIRE, and BELLA: for keeping my dome warm and covered, for helping me feel feminine and allowing me to continue my familial finger/hair-twirling habit, for allowing people to see me and not my bald head, for not taking it personally when I want to go bald, and for helping me avoid scaring small children.

I'd like to thank all of you fabulous products—I simply could not do this without you!

Our Scars

Tina Rotolo
October 2012

When I was sixteen years old, my mother brought me into her bedroom to show me the results of her radical mastectomy. A collapsed, sunken chest wall where her breast used to be, haphazardly "patched" with a skin graft from her thigh, the skin a darker shade—a reddish-brown with staple scars from her surgery. I remember being angry at the doctors for disfiguring my mother. They put her back together like a pumpkin-patch scarecrow. And scare me it did; it scared the shit out of me. I spent the next nineteen years afraid.

Fast-forward to July of 2005. I was thirty-five years old; exactly one month before my thirty-sixth birthday. I was at work that day, July 19, when my cell phone rang with the news I already knew. Living with fear for nineteen years had prepared me for the words my surgeon delivered that day.

I had a prophylactic bilateral mastectomy (there was confirmed cancer only in my right breast) on August 17, 2005. I met with a plastic surgeon for a preliminary consult a week prior to my mastectomy. He discussed all my options and told me that I had until moments before I went under to make my decision. Did I want immediate reconstruction? I didn't think so. I decided to wait until I saw the results of my very competent surgeon's handywork. The bandages that wrapped my chest for two weeks after my mastectomy brought me protective comfort as the weight of the memory of my mother's scars threatened to crush my spirit. The highly anticipated day had come, and as I stood in front of my bathroom mirror, I took very slow, deep breaths as my bandages were unwrapped.

Even though the steri-tape covered my actual incisions, I could see right away that my chest was *not* sunken. I breathed my first (of many) sighs of relief. As the days and my healing progressed, I anxiously awaited seeing the scars themselves. Soon all the steri-tape was off, and I stood once again in front of my bathroom mirror. I had two pencil-thin horizontal scars where my breasts had lived for thirty-five years. They were...magnificent!

I contemplated getting some sort of warrior symbols tattooed on my chest incorporating my scars. One day at a BAYS support-group meeting I heard the bravest warrior I had ever met, Deb Mosley, say that she would never cover her mastectomy scars—that they were a fierce symbol of her fight, and she always wanted to be able to see them. Right there, at that very moment, I was moved and my mind was made up too. Today, seven years later, I proudly wear my scars with fierceness and grace—for me, my mother, and all my sisters who fight for their lives every day.

III. NAVIGATING RELATIONSHIPS

My Cancer and My Son

Laurie Hessen Pomeranz
May 2011

On the day before my mastectomy, I went to visit my Dad. I wanted to give him a hug, to reassure him I was okay, and to see in his face that he believed I'd be okay. When we said goodbye, the anguish in his eyes was unmistakable. I said, "Dad, I'm going to be fine. I'm not scared. I'm in good hands. Please, don't be scared." He gazed at me with his trademark gentleness, and said, "Sweetheart, if someone accidentally elbowed you, I'd be upset...and this is much bigger than that."

In that moment, I realized in a whole new, visceral way how much we suffer at the thought of our child suffering.

When I learned that I had breast cancer, I was dreading the pain and fear it would cause my boy, Jack. He already knew about cancer because my mother died of the disease fourteen years before he was born. I knew that in his mind he would make the association with his Grandma Bea, and imagine his mama might die, too.

My husband, Jeff, and I did not disclose the news of my diagnosis for a week or so, until we knew what the action plan would be. Then, it was time to tell our son. On a sunny Sunday afternoon, we sat Jack down and I got started. I told him I'd seen and felt a funny bump in my breast, so I went to the doctor and he took a little piece out of it, and we found out it was cancer. I would have surgery and then some very strong medicine that would make the cancer go away.

Jack stared into the distance and said, "Whoa. You have cancer?" (long pause) "Whoa..."

We explained the cancer I had was very different than the cancer his Grandma Bea had in her kidney. I was lucky because I could feel the bump and get it taken out. Grandma's cancer wasn't one you could see or feel, so no one knew until it was too late.

I looked into Jack's thoughtful blue eyes, eyes far-away and churning with new information, and I asked, "How are you feeling right now?" He stared back at me, and said, "I kind of just feel like, 'whoa...'" A long, heavy pause followed, and then, "Can we go outside and play catch now?" With a little laugh of surprise and relief, I said, "That sounds like a great idea, buddy." I was struck by my child's ability to know how much he could tolerate for the moment. After a week of diagnostic work-ups—a mammogram, CT scan, ultrasound, PET scan, MRI, and several grueling biopsies—I was bruised and scared, and playing catch was exactly what I needed to keep me feeling like life would go on. Jack was approaching and retreating from the intensity in just the way he needed, and it was a revelation to me.

Ultimately, I completed eight months of treatment that included a mastectomy, four months of chemotherapy, and six weeks of radiation. The rigors of cancer treatment impacted my mothering, and my ability to be available to Jack in all the ways I normally am. Because he's my only child, he has received the entirety of my maternal attention.

But during the exhausting months of treatment, I needed to allocate significantly more time and attention to my own needs.

I could not chaperone field trips, or be room mom at school, or play catch in the backyard, or shoot hoops at the park. We had to find new, more calm, less strenuous ways to be together. There were incisions, drains, bone pains, steroids that kept me up all night, anti-nausea meds that made me sleep all day, and radiation burns. There was no rough-housing, no getting scrappy. Jack had to be careful around me. Mama was much more delicate than usual. Before he'd lay down next to me and rest his head against my chest, he'd ask, "Can I put my head right here?"

Having cancer made me want to hold fast to my husband and son. Embracing my boy was even more poignant and crucial than ever. I felt physically, emotionally, and mentally calmer when he was close, and I could hold his warm, skinny body against mine. My husband described an emotion that often swept over him, to want to hold our son, and me, tighter than ever. Family snuggles became a biological imperative.

An upside of my new fragility was that we did a lot of quiet cuddling in bed, and on the pull-out couch, where we often set-up camp for dinner. Cancer made me anti-processed food and anti-empty carbs, so hot dogs and mac n' cheese were off the table. I don't recommend getting cancer for this, but an amazing by-product of my weakened state is that people cooked for us—often and fabulously. We were treated to healthy, beautiful vegetarian dinners made by an incredible, far-reaching circle of friends: our village in the big city. And, we came to deeply appreciate a new facet of Jack's adaptable personality, as he dove into plates of Chinese five-spice tofu, and Mexican quinoa salad.

For the four days after each chemo treatment, I was bed-ridden with bone pain. Jeff nicknamed me "Shuffley" for the way I would totter across the bedroom floor, to the kitchen, then back to bed. It was very difficult to have Jack in the house during those dark days. It felt like my bones were in labor. I required a lot of silence, sleep, and pain medication to get through it.

We needed to ask for a lot of help with Jack. He went for sleepovers and play-dates far more often than usual, and with a wider range of friends and family than ever before. I came to know and respect Jack's sense of adventure in a whole new way, as I watched him pack up his little SpongeBob wheelie bag and head out with wide eyes and enthusiasm to a medley of different homes. He always came back with funny stories to tell about his friends' little brothers and sisters and their antics, especially at the dinner table.

Letting Jack go, trusting that he could feel safe, happy, and secure with so many caring people, was probably as valuable a learning experience for us as it was for him. We had to let him go, and be ready to receive him — to give him a sense of home and stability when he returned. It was good preparation for the rest of our life as parents.

At the one-year anniversary of my diagnosis, my cancerversary, I asked Jack what he thought had been different about the previous year, when I was sick. He said, "You couldn't play sports with me...but now you're better!" I am indeed. It feels like a miracle.

Makes me want to go outside and play catch.

The Phantom Menace

Ann Kim
October 2012

My sons were three and seven when I was diagnosed with breast cancer. In those frantic first days after diagnosis, the thing that worried me the most—more than surgery, chemo, or radiation—was how to tell the kids. Thankfully, the nurse-practitioner who called with the results of my fine-needle aspiration biopsy had the wisdom to schedule two back-to-back appointments for me: first, with a breast surgeon, and then with a psychologist.

Dr. P. had a straight-talking, no-nonsense approach that suited me perfectly. "So, what can I help you with? What's on your mind?" I asked her advice on how to tell my kids about my cancer. She told me that children my kids' age don't have any preconceptions about cancer, and that they are primarily concerned about themselves. Will their day-to-day life change? If so, let them know. "Mommy won't be able to take you to preschool anymore but Daddy will," or "I need to go to the hospital for a couple days, but Grandma will come over to take care of you."

She told me to be truthful and not to sugar-coat or use euphemisms. "Don't call your cancer a boo-boo or say it's like a cold. Kids get boo-boos and colds. If you say it's like a cold and then all your hair falls out, it's confusing to them. Your kids may wonder: will my hair fall out if I get a cold?" She said not to overwhelm the kids with unnecessary details. "You don't know how you'll respond to chemo. You might do great, you might not. There's no need to tell them right now that you'll be throwing up. If and when that happens, you can just tell them the medicine is making you feel sick, which will be the truth."

Then I asked the $64,000 question, the one I was afraid to ask myself: What if they ask me if I'm going to die? What do I tell them? "First of all, they probably won't ask you. Again, they have no preconceptions about cancer. But if they do ask, you need to be honest. Tell them that it's something serious, but that the doctors are going to work hard to make you fine. That's probably all they need to hear."

It took me a few weeks to get my treatment plan finalized and to summon up the courage to talk to my boys. My husband and I called them into the dining area.

"Remember when Mommy went to the doctor? Well, the doctor told me that I have something called cancer, and it's pretty serious. It means I have some bad stuff in my body, so I need to go to the hospital for a day or two so the doctor can take it out. It's like when we play the game Operation. That's what the doctor will do: operate and take the bad stuff out of my body."

My sons seemed moderately interested so far. But I knew I would have to go through chemo, and to explain that, I needed to bring out the big guns—literally.

Like many boys their age, my sons were obsessed with *Star Wars*, especially *Episode I: The Phantom Menace*.

"Cancer is like the battle in *Star Wars* with the Droid Ships.

When the doctor operates and cuts out the bad stuff, it's like when the Gungans shoot at the Droid Ships. But even if the Droid Ship is destroyed, is Naboo safe? What do you think might have happened?" I held my breath: was this too complicated an analogy for them?

"Some of the droids might have escaped?" Jonah, my older one, replied. "Yes!" I said with relief. "Yes, exactly; some of the droids might have escaped. And that's what might happen with my cancer. Even though the doctor destroys the Droid Ship, a few bad droids might have escaped and gone to my toe, or my tummy, or even my brain. So Mommy will need to take some strong medicine called chemo, which is like these awesome Jedi who will go out and hunt down every droid to make sure they don't cause trouble."

My kids were fascinated. Their Mommy was like a *Star Wars* battle zone, with good pitched against evil.

"But what happens when a Jedi runs around really fast and tries to shoot droids?" I asked. Jonah paused thoughtfully: "They might hit the wrong things?" "Yes!" I said, again with relief. "Even though chemo is pretty awesome, it can also be a little dumb. It shoots everything that grows fast, because cancer grows fast. But other things, like hair, also grow fast. That means the chemo is going to accidentally shoot my hair cells, so all my hair will fall out."

At this point, my three-year-old Theo, who had been rapt with attention this whole time, suddenly burst out laughing.

"Bald! You're going to be bald! That's funny, Mommy." And it *was* funny, so we all laughed.

Happy Bald Day

Nola Agha

As a mom, I spend a lot of time (well, most of my time) making breakfast, making lunch, driving to school, doing art, playing games, making dinner, running baths, reading books, washing clothes, sewing Halloween costumes, and the list goes on and on. All parents know what kind of energy is needed to make it through a day.

So imagine my shock and surprise in November, 2010, when a sore breast, then mammogram, then biopsy resulted in a stage-III breast-cancer diagnosis. My kids were two and three years old. I spent the first few weeks in shock, horror, and sadness, trying to wrap my head around what the future meant: Would I die? Would my children have a mother? Would my husband be a single father? How would we plan for the future? How would I get better? Once the shock passed, I mentally grounded myself in a positive attitude. I was going to do everything possible to live, and I was not going to die. That was my stance, and I never wavered from it.

While the diagnosis was a blow, the treatment can best be described as a marathon. Weeks and weeks of physically and mentally debilitating treatments left me unable to care for myself or my children. At one point, I was taking thirty-three different medicines. And since they left me mentally fuzzy, weak, and mostly incoherent, it took a very well-organized spreadsheet to help my caregivers figure out when I needed to take what.

Although I struggled daily with the physical pain of treatment, I also struggled daily with the guilt of a mother. I couldn't stand up long enough to make a peanut-butter-and-jelly sandwich. Really think about that. Then think about all of the other tasks that you do for your kids that only require sixty seconds. I couldn't do any of them.

Bone pain made it impossible to get down on the floor to play with trains or dolls. My children, now so accustomed to hearing me say I wasn't feeling good enough to play, asked me questions like, "Mommy, will you ever be able to play again?" It broke my heart. My daughter, just two, didn't know her ABC's, couldn't count to ten, and every day my guilt grew as I realized she was being shortchanged in her cognitive development.

While doctors can now do amazing things to save a person's life, there is little they can do to help with the daily reality of life with kids. Some days I would see two or three different doctors. None allowed children into their offices (due to the needles, chemicals, and other nastiness), never mind the fact that I needed assistance to get myself to the car, someone to drive me, and there was no way I could have gotten two kids dressed and buckled up. So, each day I had to figure out who was taking care of the kids, who could help, and how to use my waning energy to explain my absence to two crying, sad little kids.

Through the emotional, mental, physical, and logistical challenges, we constantly tried to keep the kids involved, engaged, and aware. I learned this lesson very early on. After I started chemo, I got a haircut in preparation for my impending hair loss. I left home with long, long hair and came home with a pixie cut. The kids were startled, unsettled, and confused. My son announced that he hated it. Although I tried to explain that I did it because I was about to lose my hair, they didn't understand why I did it without them. At that point, I realized we had to tell them (almost) everything and prepare them in advance for what was to come.

The morning finally came when I lost about a quarter of my hair in the shower. It would have been more if the hot water hadn't run out. The hair just kept coming and coming. It was such a royal mess that we decided it was time to shave it all off.

That afternoon my husband went out and bought clippers and a cake and we had a haircut party. The kids held the clippers, felt the vibrations, and even helped shave a few strips off my head. We cut a mohawk, laughed about it, and then cut that off too. At the end, we put candles on the cake and sang, "Happy haircut to you, happy haircut to you..." When that was done, we sang, "Happy Bald Day to you..." All in all, it was a success, and my son even announced that he liked my new haircut.

After that we really made an effort to engage the kids in big events. Before my first mastectomy, we role-played "surgery." We pulled out all of their stuffed animals, a big box of Band-Aids, and pretended they were the doctors. They performed surgery on their patients and then put Band-Aids on when they were done. I was the nurse that made sure no one hugged the animals in the same place where they had Band-Aids—this way when I got home after surgery they could see my "Band-Aids" and know right away that they couldn't hug me in those places. Instead, I got lots of leg and wrist hugs.

At the end of the day, this is a nightmare journey for any person going through it. The extra challenge for parents is to somehow guide your kids through it too—trying to make sure they are taken care of, involved but not scared, while simultaneously managing your guilt and fear. But because there have been so many parents before me struggling through cancer treatment, there is at least a fantastic pool of ideas, like haircut parties and role-playing, to help everyone make it through together.

Birthday Trip

Chi Hammer
August 2010

For months, I have been thinking about taking a road trip with my kids. I wanted to drive down to Monterey Aquarium, make my way up to Santa Cruz, and then drive up Highway 1 to Año Nuevo State Park to see the elephant seals, stopping at beaches along the way. I figured it would take three days.

When I finally decided that I was feeling healthy enough to actually pursue this adventure, it was very exciting. And then four days before we were to leave, I experienced very severe side effects from my new chemo regimen, Zometa.

The nurse had warned me that some people experience side effects, especially on the first infusion, but she claimed it was "very rare." I thought to myself, "so far in my cancer life, I've seemed to have fallen in that 'very rare' percentage." But I tried to be positive and focused on a smooth infusion. That night, the severe reactions began and lasted two days. I pretty much checked off the entire list of possible side effects. I wasn't sure if this trip was going to happen.

But I figured if I was strong enough to talk, walk, eat, and drive again then I should go for it. The hotels were already booked and not refundable. I looked at the physical challenges as a genuine reminder in life that I have to enjoy what health I have while I have it. The hardest thing with chemo and fighting side effects is the inability to be with my kids and interact with them. If the ball rolls toward your corner, you gotta run with it. So I did.

The drive to Monterey was long, but we managed to have fun singing songs and I got a great picture of the boys sharing some chocolate milk with huge smiles. It was off to a great start. We spent three hours at the museum and had a fantastic time. Then we took a long walk along the beach and saw seals. We got lost and caught dinner late but we had an awesome time having my birthday dinner at Benihana.

Growing up, it was a special tradition in my family to go to Benihana on our birthdays. Something about drinking virgin strawberry daiquiris in a funny-shaped cup and seeing the chef doing special tricks made it so exciting. I think that is a family tradition I will start doing with the kids.

I think this trip is about passing on and sharing some of my favorite things with them: Benihana, beaches, Santa Cruz Boardwalk, UCSC campus, and Monterey Aquarium. We had a blast.

It was truly refreshing to go trotting about with no schedule, errand lists, to-do lists and housework. All I had to focus on was being with my kids and that turned out to be the best present I could ever ask for. We took detours and I let them bend the rules a little and the result was absolute, authentic connection.

The kids won lots of prizes and went on many rides on the Boardwalk. I even went on one ride with them (one that turns you around and around). I screamed the whole time but the kids were so happy that it was worth it, even when I threw up later. According to Avi, his favorite ride was "the one mommy got sick on."

I showed them the UCSC campus and shared some of my memories as a student there (for two years). Showed them my favorite spot to lie on to watch clouds. We looked at the mural wall at Merrill College and I pointed out the murals that have survived since I was there twenty years ago. I showed them the spot I had won to do my own mural eighteen years ago and we took pictures of them in front of their favorite murals. The kids really enjoyed hearing my stories and linking them with something tangible.

On my birthday, we went to see the elephant seals. We were a little unprepared for the hike (1.5 miles each way) and did it without bringing any water or food. The walk back was painfully whiny and long. But I think the kids learned an important lesson: we are not always prepared for the journeys we take, and yet we will survive them with determination and resilience. We had a great lunch afterwards and the kids slept all the way back. We came home to birthday cupcakes from my mother-in-law and songs with my husband. Then I went to bed, opting to skip out on a birthday dinner.

The trip really changed my feelings about birthdays and what they mean. Each new year, we should face them with an adventure, a dare to do something different and out of the ordinary. That would be the best way to welcome a new age, as if to declare that we are ready for new perspectives, possibilities, and experiences. Life is about growing, evolving, and incorporating the new with the old.

Since the trip, I have noticed something different between my kids and me. There is a new sense of closeness and trust. It is as if they have bought in to journey with me. I can see them now, with their rolling backpacks in tow, ready to go wherever I take them, trusting that I am leading them toward something fantastic.

Many times in the past week I have looked at their backs as they skip and run in front of me. I think to myself, "Isn't life just wonderful!" I catch myself looking hard at them as if trying to encapsulate this very moment of pure happiness and contentment in an invisible bottle. I could just see their outlines forming into teens and into men.

And I say to myself, "Wouldn't it be something to see." It certainly is something worth fighting and living for. All the adventures that lie ahead, all the places our rolling luggage takes us, all the moments we have with our loved ones — every day, a different journey unfolds.

This I will keep close to my heart, to sustain me for all the hard moments that have yet to come. I know in those hard battles between chemicals and cancer, this little trip of mine will give me strength to overcome them.

So, I will be able to stand up after each battle and look forward to yet another trip, another adventure with my kids. In those dark, murky days, I will see my kids with their rolling back packs, facing me with their shining eyes, saying "Where to now?"

Out of the Ostrich Life

Chi Hammer
June 2011

In my support group, we refer to the period of our lives we spend pretending cancer doesn't exist as "the ostrich life." There is something extremely comforting about burying your head deep under the sand. Sometimes we do it in order to survive.

And for me, I wanted to forget for a while.

To pretend that my life isn't built on shaky ground.

To pretend I don't feel so much pain in my joints and muscles that it is hard for me to walk after I sit for awhile.

To pretend that I don't see women I've learned to care for and love lose the fight and die around me.

To pretend that I can spend my time rushing around doing errands and volunteering gigs like other moms.

To pretend that my future is secured.

To pretend that I never knew the meaning of cancer.

I may have stayed buried in that sand for the rest of my life, if not for my son, Avi.

One day, while Avi and I talked about our dear friend Mark's wedding in Memphis (our trip was coming up), he reached over and put his hand on my shoulder. It stopped my talking. He looked very serious and gentle at the same time. He said, "Mommy, I really, really wish that you will be at my wedding someday."

He got me.

I had to hold back the choking tears and say, "Me too, Avi. Me too. I really hope I will too."

Boom, head out of the sand. Had to excuse myself to the bathroom, so I can cry me a river.

I started to evaluate my situation and strategize a solid plan of survival. I started to read cancer-fighting books and I went back through my cancer history to analyze the factors that made me survive chemo. I came up with a two-pronged approach: spirituality and food.

I started with spirituality but quickly realized I couldn't tap into it. The antidepressant I was on had somewhat frozen my emotions. My feelings seemed disconnected and artificial. So I gradually lowered my dose until I was able to stop completely. Then I learned to experience all my emotions again, completely new. As if I had lost my sense of taste and all the flavors came back one at a time.

Sadness is a flavor that lingers and haunts.
Happiness is cotton candy, sweet and fleeting.
Loneliness is a lemon lollipop, something you don't share with others.
Fear is a spicy dish that tears up your stomach and leaves you in anguish for days.
Surprise is like pop-rocks, bursting inside.
Love is a cup of hot chocolate on a winter's morning.
Peace is green tea in a cozy cafe.

As I experience emotion again, I start to reconnect with my body. I start to feel and understand all the side effects of the medicine, the chemo experience, all the weight gain, and what was left after the surgery.

The next step is food. How to replenish this wounded earth that is my body so I can rebuild and plant that garden of flowers I saw at the beginning of this battle. I have been reading up on macrobiotic food and other plant-based diets. It is clear where I must go in order to up my survival rate. I am finally ready to take that next step. And no one is happier than my health-nut husband, who is waiting with outstretched arms and a smile as I inch toward a more sound lifestyle.

Ignorance is not bliss. It is only a clear head and vision that will lead me to Avi's wedding someday. Hopefully, the "after he graduates from high school, college, lands a well-paying job, meets the love of his life and no babies yet" kind of someday. I can wait.

Unconditional Acceptance

Sarah de Haaff
August 2012

I couldn't help but notice the (barely) eighteen-year-old girl next to me this morning at The Bar Method. She was all spunk and energy and fresh-faced enthusiasm. Next to her I felt old and tired.

It feels like all of a sudden *everyone* is younger than me. The "old" Olympians are still younger than me. I remember going to Giants' and A's games and thinking the players were so old. Now they are all younger than me. How the heck did that happen?

Someone referred to our group of friends as in our "late thirties" and I flinched. Then, a friend at my twenty-year high-school reunion said we were "almost forty" and I wanted to punch her. I am NOT almost forty. I'm still twenty-eight. Yeah that's right, in my head ten years ago, I was only eighteen. Not twenty-eight. There is just absolutely no way I am turning thirty-eight next month.

That's just plain wrong.

Which makes it *super* confusing that I just went to my twentieth high-school reunion!

I am not old enough to stand around at a high-school reunion talking about how old we are.

Uh-uh. Not yet.

Somehow though, it is particularly hard to stay in denial when there is an energetic eighteen year old working out next to you. I was annoyed. She was making it really hard to concentrate.

I think of myself as doing really well despite and in addition to all that I have gone through this year. The Bar Method is really freaking hard and there I was, powering through, trying to focus on my form. I was concentrating on making tiny purposeful movements and all I could see was her hyper, flailing body in my peripheral vision. You are supposed to move "down an inch, up an inch" and she is practically moving a foot and a half in each direction.

Slow down, Wonderwoman.

I started to close one eye, so I could block her out of my line of vision and not have to watch her spazzy, bouncy body enthusiastically embracing every move instead of wincing in agony like the rest of us.

Seriously chica. Stop bouncing. That's really fucking annoying.

And then, all of her bouncing started to take its toll, and she began to peter out halfway through each exercise. I wanted to take her by the shoulders and shake her.

Stamina, kid. Calm down. You gotta pace yourself.

Sheesh.

But then, it occurred to me that I was, in fact, kicking her butt. This chemo girl (and, OK, OK, almost thirty-eight-year old) was able to outlast the bouncy teenager. She may have looked fabulous doing it, but she wasn't able to do as many reps as I was. And man, is she gonna be sore tomorrow!

I hope.

I have learned quite a bit about stamina over the past year. Pacing myself and getting ready for each next step. These days I'm sort of fixated on mastering the art of when to push myself and when to slow down and take care of myself. I have definitely not arrived yet, but I seem to be getting quite a few opportunities to practice.

My twentieth high-school reunion just happened to fall on the eve of my one-year cancerversary. The day I heard, "I'm sorry but it *is* cancer" and received the official diagnosis. August 5th, 2011.

I wasn't sure how I felt about it and didn't want to make too big a deal of it. But I noticed I was feeling way more anxious about my reunion than I should have been, and I am pretty sure it had a lot more to do with the upcoming cancer milestone than the reunion itself.

My husband Greg watched, completely perplexed, as I started to unravel.

First, I decided to try a cleanse. Initially to help rid my body of leftover chemo and radiation toxins. But also to help neutralize all of the eating and drinking I did for two weeks with my cousins in Missouri. And if, for some reason, on the off chance, I just so happened to lose one or two of the twenty cancer-treatment pounds that I've gained this year...well, you wouldn't hear me complaining.

Then, I got a massage. I thought it would help me relax. And it did. Temporarily.

Then I decided I needed a facial! *Yes, that's it. That would make me feel good.* That would totally take my mind off the fact that I really miss my long hair and my real boobs. It would absolutely help me feel better about not fitting into any of the clothes in my closet.

And then the woman doing my facial recommended an extra-special fancy oxygen facial that would rehydrate my skin and she would throw in some micro-dermabrasion for free to take off a few layers of dead skin that I had...*Yes, that sounds perfect!*

Yes! Make me beautiful again! Or just bring me back to normal. I'll totally settle for that.

Last year at this time I was in super-duper shape, feeling strong, self-confident, enjoying my long red hair, even making it more red at times. Gone were the days of feeling insecure about anything. I was happy with my body and feeling healthy. I was in my mid-thirties and doing a pretty good job of accepting myself unconditionally.

I remember feeling like I wanted to shake things up and bring more excitement and color into my life. Things definitely got very exciting, but not exactly in the way I meant. I meant more dancing and music and color and creativity and fun! I meant now that I had this parenting thing down (yeah, right) I was going to start taking really good care of myself and only committing to things that brought me joy! What a difference a year makes!

Fast forward...now I have this mop of very short, very curly, dark brown hair. I am bigger in different places than ever before, and smaller in some interesting new places. The arm without any more lymph nodes is still numb in some spots and just looks different. My dark under-eye circles are fading, but my face looks older now. I see pictures of me and it still takes me a second to register that the one in the middle with the short dark hair and round face is actually me.

My husband is absolutely fabulous. I love him, but he will just never be able to fully understand the feeling of suddenly not fitting into your clothes. He is a man and has the metabolism of an athlete. I swear all he has to do is think about going for a run and he loses weight.

So my friend Shonnon came over armed with several fun dress options for me to try on. Love her! Finally, someone who understood getting prepped for a reunion. She didn't think it was odd at all that I was diving into this whole crazy beauty ritual. Didn't bat an eyelash when I stripped down and started trying on outfits.

I chose something I felt good in. I didn't care if it was too dressy, or not interesting enough...who cares? This was for me.

The next day, on a whim, I went and had my make-up done. But all of this pampering was making Greg a little nervous.

"Um, do you think it's still OK if I wear jeans?"

"Yes honey, all of this is not *really* about the reunion. It's in Berkeley. Enough said. And it's at the Down Low. Jeans are more than fine."

People kept saying to me, "If other people are judgmental, it's their problem, not yours." But that's not it. I was not worried about other people judging me. It was about me. I needed to accept myself for where I was and what I looked like. And I hadn't gotten around to that yet.

It's easy to do that when things are going well, harder to do when you don't recognize the image you see in the mirror. And until last week, I don't know if I had fully embraced the new me. I mean, I barely looked in the mirror when I was bald. I would look quickly to take out my contacts or pencil-in eyebrows, only focusing on a small feature instead of the whole picture. It's like I held my breath and waited for that part to be over. It was too disturbing to process, so I didn't.

And even now, when I dream, I still have long, red hair. My identity has always been wrapped up in being a redhead. Thirty-six years as a redhead is hard to shake. Yes, I know I can totally dye it back to red, but somehow it's not the same.

People did not recognize me at the reunion.

It made the whole thing very amusing. I had to say, "Sarah Haberfeld" to people when saying hello. And then watch their face as the recognition began to dawn on them. We had our high-school-senior photo on our name tag, so I just started holding that up and smiling, waiting for it to register. I got really good at bracing myself and waiting for the reaction.

"Oh my gosh, I didn't recognize you at all, your hair is so short! It looks great!" And my favorite, "What made you decide to cut it all off?"

"Ummm...Well..."

And I couldn't exactly lie. That felt too weird. What was I gonna say, "Just a whim?" "Got attacked by some scissors?" That felt inauthentic, so I just told them.

If they had just said, "it's so short" or "I love it," I would have said "thank you." But when they asked a direct question, I had a hard time not fessing up.

One of my favorite moments was when I saw my high-school-bestie-turned-college-ex-boyfriend. I was on auto-pilot, and as I approached him, I was just about to say my full name again when he gave me a big smile and hug. Not the fake kind other people were giving me until they figured out who I was. No, this was the real, *I-know-who-you-are* kind of smile. And when I said something about people not recognizing me, he looked at me like he couldn't believe it, and that it was crazy talk. I can't remember what he said exactly, but something to the effect of, "Well, of course I recognize you—you have the same face!"

Totally made my night. Because in that moment, everything inside of me relaxed. He's right. Thank you, Joe. For reminding me that, yes, I am absolutely still me. My face is the same—my eyes, my smile, my voice—all still the same and the people that really matter will see that and know who I am.

My identity can be flexible. I think that is the "unconditional" part of loving oneself unconditionally. Greg joked that it seemed like I was getting ready for my wedding. And maybe I was. I was kind of remarrying myself. Saying "I do" to this new version of myself. Vowing to accept myself—the good, the bad, and the ugly. No wait, that's not it. For better or worse. In sickness and in health.

Yeah, that's it.

And trust me, it's still changing. I really shouldn't get too comfortable with what I look like now. I still have to have one or two more surgeries. People say post-chemo hair changes can be temporary. My weight might fluctuate some more.

And I will just try and breathe through it.

It's been a cuckoo kind of year. With many, many lessons. One thing I've definitely learned this year is that any given moment might suck, "this too shall pass" and it will probably change again. I know deep down where it matters, nothing has really changed. I am still me, and my life is really good.

Stamina kid. Calm down. You gotta pace yourself.

Super-Sad, Sweet (Hopefully) Love Stories

IPJ

Dating with metastatic breast cancer is hard. Seriously, what am I supposed to write on my online dating profile? I have moments when I'm not sure I would date myself. A friend who is also thirty-something, hot, athletic, fun, and outgoing dated a guy who said she had too much baggage: breast cancer, divorced, and with a child. That's what you think people will say, right? Amazingly, nobody has said that to me yet.

When I was bald, guys hit on me. Way more than B.C. (before cancer). I would say, "I'm bald. Do you know what that means?" They said whatever, they didn't care. I didn't think I could be attractive while bald. It was such a great boost to my fragile ego.

A few years later, after the cancer spread to my liver, I decided to try and have a baby. Not in my body, because my tumor grows with estrogen, so carrying a baby would kill me. I hired a surrogate and used the embryos I froze when I was first diagnosed. Embryos made with my eggs and an ex-boyfriend's sperm. In the middle of this process, I met a beautiful man who said he wanted to be with me. He knew I had cancer. He knew I was trying to have a baby using my ex's sperm. Some serious baggage he's taking on here.

After about a month of dating, the shit hit the fan. On the last try to implant my embryos, she was pregnant. For a week. Then she miscarried. The beautiful man came with me to the final appointment with the surrogate. It hadn't worked. All my embryos were gone. I cried; I ate sushi. That's what I do when I have a bad day. Eat very expensive raw fish. Then I told the beautiful man that I had more tumors in my liver. I was going to have liver surgery the next month. I said, "This is my life, are you sure you want to walk this path with me?" He said, "Bring it on."

Fast forward a year and a half. I stayed with beautiful man for a year but it ran its course. I met a new guy. The important thing to know here is that treatment for estrogen-sensitive cancer means being put into menopause. Yep, at thirty-four years old, I'm in menopause. No hormones. It's hard on the libido, as well as a few other things. The following story is sad and funny and totally X-rated, so don't read if you're under twenty-one or not in menopause…

This guy is super sweet and considerate. After getting to know each other for about a month, finally we have sex for the first time. Suddenly I'm bleeding! From a woman who hasn't had a period in three years, WTF?! Must be due to serious vaginal dryness and not enough lube used. But it's a guy's worst nightmare, right?

Then, in the morning, I wake up at 5 a.m. feeling sick and I run to the bathroom—it's coming out both ends at once. I'm a mess. I lay on the bathroom floor for a few hours. The guy asks if he can help me; I say no, but I'm really sorry if I'm contagious and he starts puking in two days. He leaves. Poor guy, I hope he still likes me. He already thinks I'm a train wreck, and I just proved it!

How can I explain that this is not normal for me? Then I think about it, and sometimes my life is very much like that. Shit coming from every orifice.

Amazingly, the sweet guy calls again, and stays with me, though it still hurts and bleeds a little when we have sex. I use estrogen cream and the Estring, but I still have an eighty-year-old vagina in the body of a thirty-four-year-old woman. I hope the sweet guy continues to handle me—all of me—gently.

My Recent, Bizarre, and Slightly Gross Day: A Mets Story

Sacramento Susan

Having metastatic breast cancer that is hormone sensitive, I lived the past fourteen years without one drop of estrogen—no ovaries, no hormone replacement, nothing. Menopause overnight, at the age of thirty-four. Yes, it sucks, it's as bad as it sounds.

I always dreamed and joked that when my anti-hormone therapy no longer worked, at least I could score some estrogen as a possible treatment. Well, after many long-awaited years (and I'm not complaining that I got all those years), the day came; although it seems counter-intuitive, I was able to take high-dose estrogen. I was on cloud nine, sexting my husband from the doctor's office of the good news, and anticipating a reprieve from the extreme vaginal dryness, hot flashes, insomnia, and all that comes with medically induced menopause.

At first, all was well and I actually had to wear mini pads due to all the wonderful clear fluids flowing from my va-jay-jay. Personal lubricants—gone! No longer needed! Life was great. Flying along on my bike, I felt like Superwoman in every way. It was the dream I had envisioned for fourteen years.

Well, then a funny thing happened on the way to the best cancer treatment ever imaginable...I got a blood clot at the tip of my thirteen-year-old portocath inside my vein, causing my face, neck, and arms to swell up. To treat this, I was given blood thinners. After starting blood thinners, the next day I began to experience vaginal bleeding—and bleeding...and bleeding...and bleeding. I blew through box after box of super-plus tampons with no end in sight.

The next day, I saw my doctor and she sent me for a blood test. My port was broken so they drew it traditional-style from my veins. I stood with my arm under warm water for some time and then took my seat in the chair where they pull down the bar (almost like you are on a roller-coaster). I told the lady, "I need to go to the bathroom," and she told me, "you can't because your arm will get cold." Again, I calmly repeated, "you don't understand...I need to go"; she said, "well, you have protection on, don't you?" I could feel the warmth in my groin, but not the warmth often described in a Harlequin romance...rather, the kind which forced me to watch TV all day on a plastic bag to protect the couch.

I was finally freed from the chair after the blood was drawn from my arm, ran to the bathroom (literally two feet away), and gushed blood—all over the floor, down my legs, on my flip-flops, everywhere. I tried to clean it up, but every time I moved, I was stepping in blood and leaving it in my footsteps. The bathroom looked like a crime scene. My darling husband came to check on me; we put my flip-flops in the sink and rinsed all we could. We let the front desk know, "the bathroom floor is covered in blood and we were unable to clean it up." They just shrugged and said "OK," like it was something they heard everyday.

On the way home, we stopped and bought the newly advertised Depends "Silhouettes." I was the happiest and most confident person you ever saw in a pair of Depends! I thought they were genius. No shame here.

About My Mother

Carolyn Helmke

As posted to the BAYS list-serve, Monday, July 23, 2012 9:34 pm:

Hello all,

I have been thinking that many of you don't know about my Mom and her breast cancer story. There are a few things that I want to share.

My Mom was diagnosed with breast cancer in 1969 when I was five. She had a mastectomy with something like seventeen nodes affected. Now, this is not a good diagnosis. But my parents got through it, and my Grandma came, and it seemed kind of like a party to me (because my Grandma was quite a hostess and really, really loved kids), and they felt like they had beaten it and then moved on.

When I was in the second or third grade, my Mom had a second mastectomy. Again, many lymph nodes affected. My parents got depressed, because they realized that cancer was here to stay and started worrying.

My Mom kind of hated her oncologist. He was this guy who gave more information to my Dad than my Mom and pretty much told her to work on her will. So they knew this guy at our church and asked him what he thought of her oncologist. He acted like a good ol' boy (even though we are uptight Presbyterians, not swaggering Southerners), and said his buddy, my Mom's oncologist, was a "fine man," and they should be happy to have him for a doctor.

So my Mom went to the university library (we lived in Ann Arbor, Michigan) and researched all of the doctors. She found an oncologist, who happened to be a woman, who seemed to have access to new treatments. My Mom hooked up with her, had her ovaries removed, and went on Tamoxifen. (Chronology a little messy here, but she was definitely one of the first people to get Tamoxifen.) Let's just say it was sometime in the seventies.

It is hard to say exactly when my Mom's cancer metastasized, but I am guessing around 1973 or so. Probably earlier. Don't forget about all the cancer in those lymph nodes! And she had no chemo after her treatment, just radiation.

My Mom died in 1984. So for at least ten years she had metastatic cancer and many periods of remission. I am not going to get any of the dates straight, but there were mets to her bones, lungs, and, I believe, her liver. Maybe not. I may be making that up.

I'm telling this story because it is such a reminder that the cancer path is an unpredictable one, and metastases can live for a very long time in a person's body.

Love all of you!

Carolyn

IV. GRIEF AND GRATITUDE

Pity Party

IPJ
November 2010

Tomorrow is my thirty-sixth birthday. My body is in rebellion. Am I young? I feel like an old lady. Except when I was out dancing last night until 3:30 a.m. Flirting, looking hot, but no kissing due to cold sore. Living with stage-IV breast cancer has its ups and downs. Lately a lot of downs, with a few ups to keep me from shooting myself.

The past month brought a host of new illnesses and a few old ones returning. I finished radiation on my little chest wall metastasis around mid-October. Then I got shingles on my right thigh. Very itchy, not too painful. Then I couldn't swallow for three brutal days, due to a burning pain in my chest. My doctor called it "esophagitis." Was starving but couldn't eat. I figure it was viral—a friend had similar symptoms a few days before me. This was right before the Halloween Gorillaz concert, which was off the hook!

Then serious heartburn struck, at a friend's band's concert. It was so bad I had to leave before they even started playing. I was drinking water and eating bread, anything to settle the acid. But I still had to go home to take my super-duper antacid. The one my doctor says will give "hospital-grade constipation" if I take it too much. Well, my "light chemo" Tykerb gives me diarrhea, so this antacid should balance it out, right?

Then a cold sore started a week later. Really? So inconvenient. And I just had shingles. Varicella *and* Herpes viruses both active.

And then folliculitis—that is, pimples all over my body, like teenage acne but without the hormones. Usually this happens from dirty hot tubs, but I hadn't even been in a hot tub. At least let me have the fun before I suffer the consequences!

And finally today, I'm feeling a general-malaise type of sick, with chills, aches all over, and a sore throat. I may have gone to bed at 4:00 a.m. (Artumnal festival was awesome. I love dressing in Burning-Man chic), but slept seven and a half hours.

My doctor says my white blood cells are normal. My immune system should be working fine. So what's up with all these "routine" illnesses lining up to knock me down?

Feeling hopeless and helpless. What can I do? How much can I take? In between illnesses, however, I will continue to live extravagantly, dancing, eating, and drinking—to the last drop.

Smiling

Julie Morgan

I love going to concerts. I could own a house in San Francisco with all the money I've spent through the years on live music. I had a double mastectomy the week of Thanksgiving and I had tickets on December 29, 30, and 31 to see Phish at Madison Square Garden. All three nights down on the floor of the arena.

The first night we were in row twelve, and New Year's Eve we were with a paraplegic, so our seats were in front but off to the side where it's wheelchair accessible. The 30th we had the best seats in the whole Garden: front-row dead-center! That night, a couple of hours into the show, my mind started to race. I remember thinking, "Wow, tomorrow's New Year's Eve and for the first time in my life, I'm *dreading* it."

I've always enjoyed the start of a new year. It was a reason to celebrate; it meant a fantastic night out with my fabulous friends; it was a night full of fun plans and an equally fun outfit. This New Year's was different. Come January, I would start chemo. A million questions were racing through my head. Should I harvest my eggs before chemo started? (I did). Should I still even consider wanting to become a mother after a diagnosis of melanoma and now breast cancer? (I do). What would I look like bald? (Hot). Would I lose my sex drive? (Nope). Dry up? (I stashed lube a few places just in case). My whole relationship with my man was founded on our strong sexual chemistry. Would I be puking all the time? (Not once). Lose more weight? (Gained some back). After my diagnosis, I went into super-detox mode and had already lost almost twenty pounds. Any more weight loss and I would look sick. Would the chemo put me into menopause? Would it damage my heart? Will the cancer come back? Was I was going to be a pale, bald, dry woman with jutting hipbones and hard fake boobs? How would I recognize myself? Who would I be?

New Year's is supposed to mean the start of something fresh, full of possibility and hope, but not this year. I did not like the sound of 2012 at all! She sounded like a real bitch. I was afraid of chemo and cancer. Afraid of what my body would look like and feel like. Then a hand shot out and grabbed my arm. The lady in the seat next to us who had been aggressively defending her front row turf throughout the show leaned towards me. "All night long I've seen you dancing with a big smile on your face! You look like you're having a blast!" And I was, despite the fears. That's what I was going to do in 2012: smile, and dance, and have a great time! I shut up those little voices inside my head for the rest of night and listened to the music.

If I Still Got My Period...

Emily Kaplan

If I still got my period, I would say it's because of PMS
That it's so hard to get out of bed.
That I want to eat every sweet thing in sight, and then every salty thing, rotating until I feel sick.
That I cried when I got home from the birthday party where I got my face painted first so Samara would be brave enough to do it.
That I can't handle it when my kids are mean to me after all I try to do for them.
That I feel sick after the other mother told me I just need to "let things go more."
That I need to go thrift-store shopping to feel better.
That I can't do more than one thing on my list of thirty things to do.
That I convince myself that walking through the aisles at Costco is plenty of exercise for the day.
That I am sure there are so many lines on my face and I look ten years older than I am.
That I want to call my friends and cry to them about how hard it is, but then I think they don't want to hear me complain, again.

Why Should It Matter?

Emily Kaplan

She asks me if I miss them
Of course I do, but I say
Not really, it's easier this way
But is it
I say no more bras
I say I had perfect boobs before
36C
That I would not want new ones
Ones that aren't really me
But why
Why am I not getting new ones
Why do people ask
Why should it matter
In so many ways I cannot admit that it does

Losses and Gains

Meaghan Calcari Campbell
October 2012

Grief is something that, unfortunately, both my husband Mike's family and my own continue to experience. I know some of you are grieving right now. My only solace is that we are grieving together.

Loss can be physical; it can also be metaphysical. I want to explore more of the metaphysical part, with excerpts from writing by the psychologists Kubler-Ross and Kessler that I was given on the topic. I promise I won't lose you on this one. You may even recognize yourself here.

Kubler-Ross and Kessler maintain that "grief is also the shattering of many conscious and unconscious beliefs about what our lives are supposed to look like."[1] We're taught, and our lives generally reinforce, the notion that if we are a good person, things will work out. If we behave well as a child, we'll get rewarded. If we eat healthy, exercise, wear sunscreen, use the crosswalk, volunteer in the community, and

---

[1] *On Grief and Grieving: Finding the Meaning of Grief Through the Five Stages of Loss* (New York: Scribner, 2005), 78.

surround ourselves with loved ones...you get the point. The rewards are things like going to college, meeting the love of your life, building a career you're passionate about, buying your dream home, getting the world's cutest kitten, and so forth. "Finally, when we are old and gray, we will invite the family over to look at old photo albums, tell each one how much we love them, and then, that very night, die peacefully in our sleep."

That's the way it is supposed to be.

But then, in a split second, whether it's a cancer diagnosis, a car accident, or natural disaster, something changes. And it was never supposed to be this way. So when these things do happen, "we not only must grieve the loss, we also must grieve the loss of the belief that it shouldn't have happened at all."

My parents didn't shield me from reality growing up, but the reality is, reality was pretty good. I mostly did as I was told. (That is, except for 99% of my high-school weekends.) I was incredibly blessed that a combination of supportive parents and family, luck, and hard work brought me to this point, or let's say to the point in my life prediagnosis. While my family has had its share of lumps, especially in the past two years, my life was on a trajectory: I was supposed to have newlywed glow; I was supposed to go to Iceland and India and everywhere else; I was supposed to lead a meeting in Vancouver. Big and small, marvelous and mundane.

Instead, my days are a schedule of pills, doctors, needles, and introspection (or bone pain, a bloody nose, no hair, canker sores, acne, dry skin, leg rashes, cracking nails, and maybe a hemorrhoid thrown in for good measure). Now, my birthdays will be included in cancer statistics. Now, having a child will become the most monitored event in history. Now, every little pain or itch will become its own drama raising the question of metastasis.

You can say I'm lucky to even be able to think of a life with no sign of disease, or "NSD" in the cancer world. I am. I know this. But I'm still grieving the loss of what my life is supposed to be.

"In the grieving process, we also need to take time to mourn the life we were supposed to have...taking time to live with the question of 'why me?' For some, the answer is 'why not me? Why should I be excluded from life's losses?'"

I shouldn't be excluded from life's losses. None of us are excluded.

Postdiagnosis (I've come to learn there is always a demarcation of before and after diagnosis), my belief system needs to heal and regroup as much as my body and soul. I need to rebuild a belief system. This is what the gobs of material I have from every cancer-support nonprofit keep referring to as the "new normal." My new normal must integrate the realities of life, living with and through cancer, but still bring me hope for the future.

So, I'm setting off on that rebuilding project. It's probably bigger and definitely more significant than any home renovation Mike and I signed up for with our old house. We can't learn it by watching HGTV, or reading it in a book, or even from talking with others who have gone through it. It's our own, and, ultimately, my own project.

In writing this, I don't want my grief to emanate out like a stone in a pond, hitting you hard with each ripple. It's not all bad—much of life is *not* cancer. I notice countless things that are delightful, quietly stunning, or smirk-inducing. We all know there are a million things like this each day that our mind just cannot comprehend because we are moving so quickly. So maybe my life, being lived at a slower and more orderly pace, can help us all remember to pause and notice these moments.

Not Cancer Vol. 1:

- Canadian Thanksgiving. I feel like I get to celebrate Thanksgiving twice.
- The more than twenty spider webs I counted in our backyard this evening. Big or small spider, the webs are equally elaborate and somehow negotiated into every nook and cranny.
- Rediscovering lipstick. Or, actually discovering it for the first time in my thirties. It can make you look better than you feel.
- Ivy, the runaway dog who came back home.
- Skyping a friend in Doha over my morning tea after she tucked her kids into bed.
- People who propose we have cat dates.
- A beautiful baby born to Alli and Reese. She looks like pure baby doll.
- Old friends and remembering why they were such a big part of my life. Because they are wonderful and loving and smart.
- All of the incredibly open and compassionate messages that make me feel so connected and lucky to have community in my life.
- My Dad and how strong he is. And how he can fall right asleep, even when he's stressed.
- And Mumford and Sons' new song, "I Will Wait for You." This one is for Mike, who is busy with work and trying to hold it all together, but still, I think he wrote this song for me. Probably both in the literal sense because I'm always late, but in the emotional sense too. And I love him for both reasons.

Hope has a funny way of creeping back in.

The World is Not Enough

Carolyn Helmke
September 2006

I got in the car and turned on the radio. I liked the song that was playing, but I quickly got itchy fingers. What if there was something better on another station? What should I do? I was enjoying the song, but…what if, what if, what if?

I have made it through the "big boys" of cancer treatment and feel relieved. And tired, and excited, and scared, and thankful. And while I would like to feel as if the whole thing is "over," I now have to live with the fact that having had cancer is not a cut-and-dried experience. Is anything in life?

I have so much recovery ahead of me, thanks to the drugs and radiation. I will still be getting Herceptin infusions every three weeks through next April. A Herceptin infusion involves a nurse sticking a needle in my port while I lie there and get drugs pumped into my veins for a few hours. It is not, I am sorry to say, a lovely cup of herbal tea at a trendy cafe.

I start Tamoxifen in a week or so. I will take this pill every day for five years if the side effects don't get me. Remember the "Freshman Fifteen"? All that pizza, beer, and ice cream that you consumed your first year of college? Well, I am now facing the "Tamoxifen Twenty." That's right, most "young" women gain twenty pounds during their first year of Tamoxifen. I am not enthusiastic about this.

But never mind my whining about the treatment. The real problem is not chemo, radiation, Tamoxifen, Herceptin, or another twenty pounds. What is truly on my plate right now is the poorly differentiated nasty beast that grew in my breasts and now lives in my mind, if not my body.

None of us know what is going to happen tomorrow. But having had cancer presents my imagination with doomsday scenarios that are not only plausible but happening to some of the incredible young women in my cancer support group.

"Yea, though I walk through the valley of the shadow of death, I will fear no evil."

I am not there yet. A huge part of my recovery process will have to be coming to terms with what might or might not be growing inside me, and then letting go of the worry and fear.

There is so much that I still want to see and do. More than anything else, I want to see all of my kids grow up. I met Antonio when he was seven, and now he is a senior in high school. In my crystal ball, I can see a day when he has a little baby and Granddad Steve is the happiest man in town. Cheryl's baby hasn't even been born, and I can already picture her first day of kindergarten, and me demanding of Cheryl that her daughter wear the dress that I gave her.

I just don't want any of this taken away from me.

I also want to see the world. So many places to go! The train to Tibet. Cheering non-doping cyclists at the Tour de France. Back to Chile. Hiking the Na Pali Coast. Visiting Cherry in Hong Kong. Biking through Indochina.

But what I really need to do is savor this moment. My dog is happily sleeping and my dahlias are stunning. My cup runneth over with love and support. I do not have to find a better song on another station. Blessings have already come my way.

September 12

Erin Hyman
September 2012

On September 12, 2001, my husband Micah and I stayed in a suite in the Venetian hotel in Las Vegas. It was huge—palatial. It had a marble bathroom bigger than my apartment at the time, with stone lions and gold-plated faucets pouring into the jacuzzi tub. The lobby, which bled seamlessly into a mall of high-end shops, had an eerily lit, faux-blue sky.

Neither of us has ever stayed at the Venetian—or any other mega-resort there—either before or since. For us, nothing ever had to "stay" in Vegas, because we simply never went there. No bachelor parties or girls weekends. No spur-of-the-moment, "Vegas, baby, Vegas!" road trips. Not even a Celine Dion concert or visit to the Guggenheim or ironic jaunt to the idyll of postmodern architecture.

We were there because a day earlier we had been in Sun Valley, Idaho, happily ensconced in my family's time-share condo, hiking and reading and watching deer walk by on the path above the river from where we were reading Levinas on the living room couch, when we got the call from my mother to turn on the television. Actually, to be accurate, when we got the call, we were asleep. We turned on the news after the planes hit but before the towers fell. After approximately twenty-four hours of watching, when airports were at a standstill, and no plane was flying anywhere in North America, we decided to drive home to Los Angeles. We were numb anyway, we might as well be staring into the blankness of the Nevada desert. There were stretches there that we couldn't even get the radio. When we drove until we couldn't drive any more that day, the place we were in was Las Vegas.

Driving in, after the shock and horror followed by sensory deprivation of the previous day and a half, we expected it to be a ghost town, empty. Or else perhaps that the whole city was grouped around various Jumbotrons down the strip, watching and waiting, crying and praying. But that was not what it was like. People were gambling. They were taking pictures of themselves in groups in front of casinos. They were eating themselves silly. They were shopping—and this was way before they were told it was patriotic to do so. In fact, the whole scene was crazy, and surreal, and unbelievably garish, and we felt like we were the only two people in the apocalypse movie who actually know that the apocalypse has come.

But looking back, it was also the moment of calm before the storm—the tsunami—of nationalism and rhetoric and jingoism and fear-mongering and legitimate grieving and all of what came after. It was so bizarre, so wildly out of tune with the horror that had just transpired, that we walked right into the middle of it and got ourselves a room, not at the Nellis Air Force Base Best Western, but at the Venetian. For when the whole world has been turned upside down, the asylum may just seem like the sanest place.

One of the feelings I remember most distinctly about that moment in time was the ominous sense of "what's next?" They say this is an element of trauma: the momentous violence has just happened, but one feels as if the worst is yet to come. Which American city was going to be bombed next? Of course, this line of thought makes our departure from our remote mountain retreat all the more irrational. But the vacation was over; we couldn't just stay out there in the evergreens and the lupine meadows; whatever happened, we needed to be back with friends and family and quite frankly, media connection. Which is why the best use we got out of that suite at the Venetian was the capability on the big-screen TV to watch several cable-news stations at once.

This year, September 12, is the day after my last chemo session. Please forgive me this heavy-handed and incommensurate analogy. I am not suggesting that any one person's illness is comparable to the events of September 11. But the coincidence of the date makes me think of the same feeling that reality has shifted in some fundamental way.

Many, many cancer survivors experience the end of treatment with dread; everyone expects them to be relieved, but it is not that simple. The damage has been done, but now you have to deal with the aftermath. I feel the same apprehension I did eleven years ago—even though the terrible has already happened, I'm waiting for the next shoe to drop. It may just get worse. That's not necessarily a factual appraisal, but it's a powerful emotional dimension. How am I to trust the body that's already deceived me once? Just like in Vegas, I may just want to yell and scream to all the indifferent, seemingly anesthetized crowds around me: "What's wrong with you? Don't you realize what's just happened?"

Of course, finishing chemo is cause for celebration, and believe me, I'm ready to throw a party. I'm tempted to plagiarize the name for it from a friend who called hers the "It-seems-like-a-dreamo-but-I'm-all-done-with-chemo" bash. I may not be in a faux gondola in the middle of the Nevada desert on September 12, but it is surreal nonetheless. There's so much yet to determine about how to establish the "new normal" on the other side. How will concerns be reprioritized? How will the passage of time be marked in new ways? How will the rebuilding begin?

I am grateful that this date falls before Rosh Hashanah. Eleven years ago, once we had returned from our stay-over in Vegas, my husband Micah (who is a rabbi) and I hosted high-holiday services at our house. It was a moment when our twenty-something friends didn't want to be at their parents' synagogue, a moment when we wanted intensely to be together in a meaningful way, but we wanted it to be personal to us.

We printed our own prayerbooks; we cleared out the furniture from the living room; we borrowed a Sefer Torah from Camp Ramah. Micah played many roles at once, but our several dozen friends all participated: chanting, leading blessings, reading texts. People brought their own poems to read; the text discussions never seemed so heartfelt, imagining death in the myriad ways of the *Unetanetokef* never so concrete; there were a lot of tears. Those services bound us to the participants in new ways that none of us have ever forgotten.

The days of awe are an amazing amalgamation of sweetness and renewal with solemnity and deep soul-searching, as we consider our own mortality. When I found out I had cancer, I had a sense of panic, of urgency, "Oh no! Not yet! Too soon!"—which is precisely the feeling that the high holidays are trying to get you to feel—"Do it now! Make a change! Don't put it off!"—without actually having the diagnosis. Or by carrying the sense that it could befall any one of us at any time.

For me, this time, the reflection on mortality won't be a mental exercise, an imaginary scenario. The touchstone of the new year will be the precise counterbalance to the disorientation of September 12. A way to acknowledge, with deep gratitude, a new start, another year of life, not in isolation in the crowd, as in Vegas, but held aloft by loving community, woven together in all our wounds, as we seek to move forward into a new phase, humbled, renewed, recommitted to what is essential.

Contributor Profiles

Nola Agha lives in the Bay Area with her husband, two children, two cats, and a turtle. She is an assistant professor of Sport Management at the University of San Francisco and a sports economics consultant. She was diagnosed with Stage-III breast cancer in November of 2010 and concluded her treatment in March of 2012.

Meaghan Calcari Campbell has roots in small-town Illinois and now calls San Francisco's Mission District home. She has worked in philanthropy, environmental science, and ocean conservation with local communities and non-profits for over ten years. Meaghan has found solace in blogging about her cancer experience. She looks forward to walks in the city, traveling further afield, and snapping photos of life at its best.

Sarah de Haaff never fancied herself a writer, but fell into it by way of her breast-cancer experience. She works with young children as a speech pathologist in San Francisco. Diagnosed in August 2011, she tackled chemotherapy, a bilateral mastectomy, and radiation, all while potty training one child and preparing the other for kindergarten. She readily admits that she could not have done it without some amazing help from her circle.

Chi Hammer emigrated from Taiwan to the Bay Area with her family when she was eight years old. She was a dedicated urban teacher at Oakland Unified School District for many years. After starting her dream job as lead coach for the New Teacher Support Department at thirty-seven years old, she was diagnosed with metastatic breast cancer. She now tends to her new career of surviving cancer treatments with the help of her husband and two active school-age sons in the East Bay. More of her writing can be found at chihammer.blogspot.com.

Carolyn Helmke was born in Michigan, went to college in Wisconsin, and has spent most of her adult life in Northern California. The love of her life is Flora the Beagle, and she thanks Angela Padilla of BAYS for making the match.

Erin Hyman is an editor of arts publications, the mother of two amazing boys, and a fierce Scrabble competitor. Her previous life as a Lit professor has made her passionate about storytelling in all its forms, and she believes that speaking the truth about our lives is essential to healing. More of her writing can be found at bmatzav.blogspot.com.

IPJ fancies herself an athlete; she snowboards, rock climbs, practices yoga, and hikes. She also loves music and dancing. She was diagnosed with breast cancer at age thirty-two, metastatic at thirty-four. She is currently NED (no evidence of disease!), living the good life.

Emily Kaplan had breastfed her five-month-old daughter the morning she was diagnosed with breast cancer. Two years after a bilateral mastectomy, Emily gave birth to a second child, a baby boy. Emily is featured prominently in the Scar Project, a series of large-scale portraits of young breast-cancer survivors shot by fashion photographer David Jay. For more information, please visit www.thescarproject.org.

As the daughter of a doctor, *Ann Kim* grew up thinking she would follow in her father's footsteps. When she realized that she couldn't stand the sight of blood, however, Ann pursued a career in law. As a founding board member and the current president of BAYS, Ann feels grateful to fulfill her childhood dream of helping people through illness, just in a different way than she had originally planned.

Julie Morgan is a nurse and an avid snowboarder. She managed to get in more than a dozen days on the mountain during chemotherapy and even fielded her doctor's phone calls (in lieu of office visits) while strapped onto her board.

Laurie Hessen Pomeranz is a San Francisco–based therapist, who works with teenage boys. She also performs with local tot-rockers Charity and the JAMband, moonlights as a jewelry stylist, and is a die-hard baseball fan. She finished chemo the day after the Giants won the 2010 World Series.

Tina Rotolo is a sixteen-year transplant to the Bay Area from Central New York. She works in Human Resources and enjoys the outdoors, as well as beautiful drives down the coast on her bright yellow BMW motorcycle.

Sacramento Susan was diagnosed with breast cancer at the age of thirty-four in 1998, and with metastatic disease a year later. She is now a retired technology consultant, was recently married, and vacations in Michoacan, Mexico as much as possible.

Dorinda Z. Vassigh enjoys walking on the beach, kayaking, and biking. She is not afraid to admit it—she likes watching TV in bed with a glass of wine and crackers. She currently practices law at Google and does pro bono work advocating for Iranian refugees. To see more of her writing visit sitforabit.mindpress.com.

Acknowledgments

We remember with love our BAYS sister Lynnly Labovitz, whose beautiful photography graces the cover of this book, and we wish to thank Amy Epstein and Jen Doan for providing the image.

Immense thanks go to Cheryl Strayed for her fierce words of encouragement to women writers and her permission to quote from *Tiny, Beautiful Things: Advice on Life and Love from Dear Sugar* (New York: Vintage, 2012).

Shout out to the incomparable Laurie Hessen Pomeranz for her eagle editing eye and unflagging enthusiasm—without her, this collection would not have made it to completion.

Lastly, we wish to acknowledge the following publications for according us the rights to republish stories that have previously appeared:

Ann Kim, "Dr. Me," *Zócalo Public Square*, May 16, 2012. www.zocalopublicsquare.org/2012/05/16/dr-me/ideas/nexus/

Laurie Hessen Pomeranz, "How We Wound Up Topless," *Salon*, Dec. 4, 2010. www.salon.com/writer/laurie_hessen_pomeranz/

———, "My Cancer and My Son," *The Mother Company*, May 12, 2011. http://www.themotherco.com/2011/05/my-cancer-and-my-son/